Science

ESL Support
Grade 3

Harcourt
SCHOOL PUBLISHERS

Orlando   Austin   New York   San Diego   Toronto   London

Visit *The Learning Site!*
www.harcourtschool.com

Contents

Strategies for Success

Throughout the United States, students with limited English proficiency and their teachers face daily challenges in the classroom. One of the greatest challenges for students is learning subjects taught in a language they have not yet mastered. The challenge for teachers is providing instruction that these students clearly understand. Academic instruction designed especially for the English language learner (ELL) meets these challenges. These strategies do not lower standards or change academic expectations for ELLs. Instead, they modify instruction to meet students' diverse linguistic and cultural needs. Through these strategies, students gain equal access to the curriculum and they experience academic success.

Rationale and Research

Research has shown that five to seven years of appropriate instruction are needed to acquire academic proficiency in a second language (Krashen, 1982). Postponing content instruction until students gain full mastery of English would be unreasonable and a disservice to these students. Educators realize that with carefully planned lessons and the use of a variety of research-based practices designed to meet the needs of ELLs, these students can meet content standards while demonstrating growth in English language proficiency.

Stages of English Language Acquisition

Proficiency Level: BEGINNER	
Pre-Production	**Early Production**
Listening/Speaking • associate utterances with meanings • use unanalyzed phrases sporadically • may need to use native language to demonstrate comprehension • respond nonverbally or with one or two words and short phrases • participate in songs, chants, and rhymes **Reading** • decode but have difficulty with English phonological awareness • comprehend simple content • begin to read single words and short phrases **Writing** • copy, label, and list • write familiar words and phrases	**Listening/Speaking** • begin to model verb tenses, such as present participles • ask and answer simple questions about familiar concepts • participate in face-to-face conversations with peers • begin to self-check and self-correct **Reading** • comprehend and recall main ideas of a simple story or other content • improve pronunciation and phonological awareness • read student-generated text **Writing** • use graphic organizers and writing frames • write simple questions and answers

Proficiency Level: INTERMEDIATE

Speech Emergence	Intermediate Fluency
Listening/Speaking • express thoughts and use original language • use complete simple sentences • produce sustained conversation **Reading** • interact with a variety of print • use writing for a variety of purposes **Writing** • transfer reading and oral language to writing • write for a variety of purposes • participate fully in editing	**Listening/Speaking** • use the listening process to improve comprehension and oral skills • clarify, distinguish, and evaluate ideas and responses • demonstrate adequate pronunciation and grammar usage **Reading** • use a variety of reading strategies • use various study skills **Writing** • use extended written production in all content areas • use adjectives, adverbs, and figurative language in writing

Proficiency Level: ADVANCED

Advanced Fluency

Listening/Speaking
- Create, clarify, critique, and evaluate ideas and responses
- Comprehend concrete and abstract topics and concepts
- Use effortless, fluent speech

Reading
- Use graphophonic cues, syntax, context, and prior knowledge to make meaning
- Read grade-level materials with limited difficulty

Writing
- Use graphophonic cues, syntax, context, and prior knowledge to make meaning
- Write to meet social needs and academic demands

Teaching Strategies

Language is learned in a variety of ways, but experience and time are important factors that foster proficiency. To acquire a second language, students must receive large amounts of *comprehensible input* (Krashen, 1982). Comprehensible input describes the understandable and meaningful language directed toward learners acquiring a second language. Language and the delivery of concepts are either decontextualized (with few clues) or contextualized (rich with clues). Traditional instruction has been very decontextualized, but English language learners rely on contextualized instruction and materials for comprehensible input (Cummins, 1994). Characteristics of comprehensible input include the following:

- Focus on communicating a meaningful message rather than on language forms
- Frequent use of concrete contextual referents, such as visuals, manipulatives, and graphics
- Acceptance of primary language use by the learner
- Minimal overt correction by the instructor
- Establishment of positive and motivating learning environments.

Language learning is developmental. When students receive comprehensible input, they progress through predictable levels of language proficiency. Students at various proficiency levels have specific characteristics and need different instructional strategies.

Teaching Strategies: BEGINNER

• Provide opportunities for purposeful listening and speaking	• Incorporate both cooperative and collaborative group opportunities
• Surround students with environmental print	• Use non-verbal role-playing
• Use rhymes, chants, songs, and games	• Incorporate visual aids, realia, or manipulatives when possible
• Group students by mixed language ability and provide for paired learning	• Use multisensory lessons when introducing new information
• Use students' prior knowledge	• Provide opportunities to apply vocabulary
• Address all learning modalities	
• Provide a low-anxiety environment	• Write key points and directions on board or chart
• Ask questions that can be answered with one- or two-word responses	

Teaching Strategies: INTERMEDIATE

- Provide opportunities for listening comprehension with contextual support
- Ask questions requiring yes/no, either/or, and listing responses
- Ask questions that require group discussion responses
- Have students label and/or categorize visuals or manipulatives
- Use patterened or predictable text
- Provide structure for writing and reading
- Incorporate shared reading and writing lessons
- Have students use numerical symbols
- Have students use a variety of graphic organizers
- Review frequently to reinforce learning

- Provide notes or outlines and use journal writing for new information
- Ask open-ended questions, and encourage students to describe, restate, and expand language
- Model mathematical concepts and conduct guided lessons using concrete models
- Use visuals, role playing, and skits to promote conceptual learning
- Focus on vocabulary/concept development
- Provide a variety of texts (genres and levels) for independent reading and concept attainment
- Encourage students to compare and contrast mathematical concepts

Teaching Strategies: ADVANCED

- Provide structure for discussions and assignments
- Guide use of reference material for research and independent work
- Provide opportunities for students to create oral and written narratives
- Provide a variety of realistic writing and speaking experiences
- Encourage creative expression
- Focus on sustained vocabulary/concept development

- Continue direct, explicit, skill instruction
- Provide opportunities for students to support and defend positions or opinions
- Model and guide students in predicting outcomes
- Provide age-appropriate reading and writing materials
- Continue ongoing language development through integrated language arts and content-area activities

Scaffolding Principles and Strategies

To encourage students to develop cognition, handle complex language tasks, and take risks, use scaffolding strategies to organize instruction. The lesson format and strategies in this book incorporate the following scaffolding principles and strategies.

Comprehensible Input

Use rich context to introduce vocabulary and concepts. Restate the content in different ways, such as simplifying the language, to help students understand the content. Speak slowly and enunciate words exactly. Avoid the use of idioms and colloquialisms. Use gestures, facial expressions, and dramatization. Use visuals such as realia, pictures, and graphic organizers. Use hands-on experience and manipulatives.

Language and Vocabulary

Explore language, clarifying how the lesson vocabulary and other words in the English language work. Explore words with multiple meanings and examine how prefixes and suffixes affect the meaning of words. Teach about the meaning of abstract terms and look at unique spellings. Teach word origins and examine compound words. Divide words into syllables or phonemes, and teach correct pronunciation and intonation by blending words.

Background/Experience

Activate and build on students' prior knowledge by accessing experience the students may already have with the content or some aspect of it. While students progress from the known to the unknown, help them make connections to previous learning. Have students describe verbally, graphically, or dramatically what they know about a topic, such as family life or concepts involving social interaction. Encourage them to brainstorm and to relate personal stories.

How to Use *ESL Support* Strategies and Lessons

The goal of this book is to teach grade-level content and to develop English language proficiency. You can modify the strategies to meet the needs of students at various levels of language acquisition. Scaffolding structures are built into each lesson and a variety of language experiences are offered. Chapter Openers and Lessons are organized in the following way.

Chapter Opener — Develop Scientific Concepts and Vocabulary

This section presents a summary of the scientific concepts, skills, and vocabulary that make up the content of each lesson in the chapter. The number of lessons in each chapter may vary.

Preview Scientific Principles

This section includes suggestions to help students become familiar with and understand the scientific principles of each lesson. A variety of motivational strategies address the different modalities of learning, such as visual, contextual, and metacognitive that are important for students learning English. The strategies set the tone for each lesson, preparing students for the activities they will encounter as they learn the concepts presented in each lesson.

Practice

An activity that focuses on the chapter topic, vocabulary words, and/or scientific principles forms the essential point for this section. Strategies are typically interactive, including the use of graphic organizers, and they accommodate different learning styles.

Apply

Through the use of poems, songs, or sentences, this section helps students apply what they learned in the Practice section. It also reinforces content while introducing and practicing language structures with students.

Lesson

① Build Background

The clock icon that begins each of the three main sections of the lesson is followed by the approximate duration in minutes of the activities in the section. The activities are suitable for at least two of the three proficiency levels (Beginning, Intermediate, Advanced) as indicated by the check marks next to each proficiency level.

Access Prior Knowledge

This section previews the concept or concepts of the lesson by encouraging discussion of the main ideas and vocabulary. The activity in this section is appropriate for at least two of the three student proficiency levels (Beginning, Intermediate, and Advanced) and serves as motivation to gain students' attention.

Preteach Lesson Vocabulary

Successful lessons for ELLs include direct instruction of vocabulary. The lesson lists the same vocabulary as the *Science* Student Edition along with several activities to reinforce the words and concepts. The activities may include suggestions to help students relate vocabulary and ideas to their experiences and backgrounds. The words should be used throughout the day and made part of students' working vocabulary. Repetition and reinforcement are essential.

Build Fluency

These strategies build and extend the activities presented in **Access Prior Knowledge** and **Preteach Lesson Vocabulary** activities. Students engage in repetition of chants, choral responses, and clapping of rhythm of words and sentences in order to develop language, practice language skills, and learn language patterns. Additional fluency-building strategies include role play or dramatization of back and forth conversations of familiar social situations.

② Scaffold the Content

Scaffolding structures are used throughout the activities in this main section in order to ensure students' success as they become exposed to and acquire the main concepts of the lesson.

Preview the Lesson

Students walk through the pages of their science text, looking at the illustrations and the main headings in order to become exposed to the focus of the lesson. You may use the headings and art to introduce and elicit predictions about the concepts of the lesson in order to present the learning goal of the lesson.

Investigate

This section provides an alternative instructional activity for the **Investigate** feature in the science text. It may include an instructional strategy that clarifies the directions or an explanation of language structures, such as idioms, that may be confusing to students as they develop their cognitive skills and learn to handle complex language tasks.

Modify Instruction—Multilevel Strategies

This section employs alternative instruction in the areas of Comprehensible Input, Language and Vocabulary, and Background/Experience, which were previously described. Interactive exercises designed to reinforce the lesson focus are provided at the Beginning, Intermediate, and Advanced levels. **For All Students** provides a way to have students apply the alternative activities under **Modify Instruction** as they continue with the lesson in their textbooks.

Extend

This section provides an extension of the **Investigate** or **Modify Instruction** activity. Students are encouraged to think about how they learn, and why what they learn is important and useful in their lives. Students will complete the **Show What You Know** page at home to demonstrate understanding of the lesson.

③ Apply and Assess

The first section under **Apply and Assess** includes a short title describing an interactive exercise which illustrates the instructional area goal of the **Modify Instruction** section. It incorporates language and concept understandings and encourages independent comprehension of ideas with peer-to-peer features.

Informal Assessment

Activities in this section check students' understanding of the alternative instructional strategies for Beginning, Intermediate, and Advanced proficiency levels under **Modify Instruction**.

Show What You Know

The blackline master in this section is intended to be reproduced as a take home sheet. It is a graphic organizer designed to have students practice and apply the concepts and vocabulary presented in the lesson. It also allows students an opportunity to summarize, review, and share with their parents what they have learned in the lesson.

Bibliography

Archibald, J. (ed.) (2000). *Second Language Acquisition and Linguistic Theory*. Oxford: Blackwell.

Bilingual Education Handbook: Designing Instruction for LEP Students. (1990). Sacramento, CA: California Department of Education.

Campbell, L., Campbell, B., and Dickinson, D. (1999). *Teaching and Learning Through Multiple Intelligences*. Needham, MA: Allyn & Bacon.

Cantoni-Harvey, G. (1987). *Content-Area Language Instruction: Approaches and Strategies*. Reading, MA: Addison-Wesley.

Cummins, J. (1994). "The Acquisition of English as a Second Language" in *Kids Come in All Languages: Reading Instruction for ESL Students*. Newark, DE: International Reading Association.

Dobb, Fred (2004). *Essential Elements of Effective Science Instruction for English Learners*, 2nd Edition. California Science Project: Los Angeles, CA.

Holt, Daniel (Ed.). (1993). *Cooperative Learning: Response to Linguistic and Cultural Diversity*. Washington, D.C.: Center for Applied Linguistics.

Krashen, S. (1982). *Principles and Practice in Second Language Acquisition*. New York: Pergamon Press.

Krashen, S., and Terrell, T. (1983). *The Natural Approach*. San Francisco: Pergamon/Alemany Press.

Mohan, B. (1986). *Language and Content*. Reading, MA: Addison-Wesley.

Randall, J.A. (Ed.). (1987). *ESL Through Content-Area Instruction*. Englewood Cliffs, NJ: Prentice Hall Regents/ERIC Clearinghouse on Languages and Linguistics. (ERIC Document Reproduction Service No. ED 283387)

Reyhner, J., Davison, D.M. (1992). "Improving Mathematics and Science Instruction for LEP Middle and High School Students Through Language Activities" in *Third National Research Symposium on Limited English Proficient Student Issues*.

Schifini, Alfredo. (1991). "Language, Literacy, and Content Instruction: Strategies for Teachers" in *Kids Come in All Languages: Reading Instruction for ESL Students*. Newark, DE: International Reading Association.

Willetts, K. (Ed.). (1986). *Integrating Language and Content Instruction*. Los Angeles: Center for Language Education and Research, UCLA. (ERIC Document Reproduction Service No. ED 278262)

Willetts, K., and Crandall, J.A. (1986). *Content-Based Language Instruction*. ERIC/CLL News Bulletin, 9 (2). Washington, D.C.: ERIC Clearinghouse on Languages and Linguistics.

1 Types of Living Things

Develop Scientific Concepts and Vocabulary

In this chapter, students will define organisms as living things. They will learn to identify the features common to all living things as well as the characteristics that make certain organisms and groups of organisms unique. They will also learn how some living things grow and change.

Preview Scientific Principles

Walk through the chapter with students, pausing to read aloud or to have volunteers read aloud the two questions that are lesson titles. Encourage students to briefly discuss each question and to tell what they already know that might help them answer the questions.

When to Use With Chapter Opener	Proficiency Levels
20 minutes	✔ Beginning ✔ Intermediate ✔ Advanced

Lesson 1: What Are Some Types of Living Things?

- Have students look around the classroom and out the window. Ask them to name things they see that might be living things. Make a list on the board.

- Call on volunteers to tell why they think the things they mentioned are living things.

- Review the list of living things on the board. If the list is short, add a variety of plants and animals to it. Point out that living things are called *organisms*. Say that the living things on the list are examples of organisms.

Lesson 2: How Do Living Things Grow and Change?

- Ask students to think about a puppy. Ask them what they think happens to the puppy during its first year of life. Explain that the puppy grows and changes over time. Say that these changes make up the puppy's *life cycle*.

- Refer to the list of organisms that students made on the board. Point out that all organisms go through a life cycle.

- Ask volunteers to tell ways that the organisms on the list change over time. (Examples: babies grow teeth; birds learn to fly; trees grow taller and bear fruit)

© Harcourt

Practice

- Have students use vocabulary from the chapter and other terms to contribute to a word web. Write *LIVING THINGS* at the center of a web on a large piece of paper. Encourage students to dictate or write characteristics of living things around the web.
- Then, have students choose words from the web to use in sentences. Encourage them to act out their sentences as they read them.

Apply

Write the sentences from the following chart on the board. Have students take turns echoing or reading a line aloud. Then, have them draw a picture to illustrate one of the lines. Direct them to create a collage on a bulletin board that posts the drawings with appropriate labels. Have students work together to choose a title for the bulletin-board collage that explains what the living things have in common.

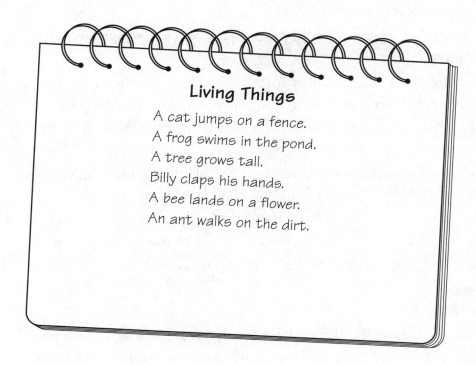

Living Things

A cat jumps on a fence.
A frog swims in the pond.
A tree grows tall.
Billy claps his hands.
A bee lands on a flower.
An ant walks on the dirt.

1

What Are Some Types of Living Things?

1 Build Background

Access Prior Knowledge

When to Use	Proficiency Levels
Before introducing the lesson	✔ Beginning
🕐 15 minutes	✔ Intermediate
	Advanced

Give students an opportunity to use sentences as they talk about living things that surround them. Ask partners to tell each other how they know that the things they mention are living things.

Preteach Lesson Vocabulary

organism, cell

Materials: building blocks

List the vocabulary words on the board.

- Have students find *organism* on page 32 and *cell* on page 34. Help them pronounce each term.

- Ask for a volunteer to stand with you. Point out that the student is a living thing. Say that another word for "living thing" is *organism*. Ask volunteers to tell what makes the student an organism. Volunteers may suggest that the student breathes, moves, or eats.

- Explain that all living things, including that student, are made up of tiny objects called *cells*. Cells are the building blocks of living things.

- Build a tower of blocks. Show how many blocks stack together to make a tall tower. Explain that many cells can work together to make living things.

- Ask students to summarize what cells are and what they do.

Build Fluency

Have students work in pairs. Direct them to talk back and forth in simple sentences. One student names an organism, and the other student tells something about that organism that makes it a living thing. Partners alternate roles and repeat.

© Harcourt

② Scaffold the Content

Preview the Lesson

When to Use With pp. 30–37	Proficiency Levels
⏱ 20 minutes	✔ Beginning ✔ Intermediate ✔ Advanced

- Ask students to point to the title on page 30 as you read it aloud. Have students observe the picture. Discuss how and where seals live. Have students compare and contrast the behavior of seals to human behavior.
- Have students preview other pictures in the lesson to identify as many living things shown on the pages as they can. Have them discuss in sentences what those organisms have in common and what makes them living things.
- Allow time for students to ask questions about pictures they do not recognize. Help them read captions to preview what the pictures show about living things.

Investigate, p. 31

Before students begin the Investigate, help them understand the phrase *not living*. Discuss that *non-* and *not* mean "no," or the opposite, so things that are "not living" do not have characteristics of living things. Help students list examples of nonliving things.

To further develop the lesson concepts, you may want to build comprehension and provide meaning for some of the other important technical words. Read aloud the words you choose, using each in a context sentence, and provide its meaning. Then have students repeat the word and find it in their texts. (*habitat*, p. 31; *reproduce*, p. 32; *energy*, p. 33; *chloroplast*, p. 35; *microscope*, p. 35)

Modify Instruction—Multilevel Strategies

Comprehensive Input The concept of living things, the focus of this lesson, involves understanding that only some things are organisms. Learners will benefit by comparing living to nonliving things. They will better understand the concept when they realize that living things have unique characteristics that nonliving things do not. The following exercises provide opportunities for students to discover ways in which living and nonliving things are different.

Beginning Have students draw and label a living thing. Ask them to show their pictures and act out something that living thing does.

Intermediate Have students copy from the board simple sentences that describe the actions of various living things. (Examples: The cheetah runs. The monkey eats.) Read each sentence aloud, having students read along or echo the sentences. Ask students to write their own sentence and act it out for the group to identify.

Advanced Ask students to list three living things. Then ask them to write a sentence that tells something all of the organisms have in common.

For All Students Start a list on chart paper of features living things have in common. As students work through the lesson, have them contribute new ideas to the list.

Extend

Have the students complete the **Show What You Know** activity on page 7 to demonstrate their understanding of living things.

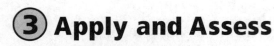
③ Apply and Assess

Make a Picture Display

Materials: magazines, glue, markers, poster board

When to Use	Proficiency Levels
With Reading Review p. 37 🕐 20 minutes	✔ Beginning ✔ Intermediate ✔ Advanced

- Have students work together in groups of three to five. Distribute the art materials.
- Have each group make two posters—one titled *Living Things* and the other titled *Things That Are Not Living*.
- Direct students to cut out pictures from magazines of living and nonliving things and then glue them on the appropriate posters.
- Ask the groups to present their posters to the class. Encourage them to explain what the living things have in common and why the nonliving things are not living.

Informal Assessment

Beginning	Intermediate	Advanced
Show pictures of living and nonliving things to the students. Have each student pick a picture of a living thing and a nonliving thing. *(Answers will vary.)*	Show students a picture of a living thing. Ask them to tell one thing the organism does to make it a living thing. *(Answers will vary.)*	Have students sort through a variety of pictures of living and nonliving things. Have them select one picture of a living thing and tell why they selected it. Have them choose one picture of a nonliving thing and tell why they selected it. *(Answers will vary.)*

© Harcourt

Chart of Living Things

Read the sentence in each row. Write *living* if the sentence describes a living thing. Write *not living* if the sentence describes something that is not a living thing.

Living or Not Living?

A **rock** rolls down a hill.	
A **rabbit** eats a carrot.	
A **tree** makes other trees.	
Dirt covers the ball.	
The **grass** grows fast.	
The **wind** blows.	

School-Home Connection: Have students take this page home to share with family members. They can use this page to tell about living things and nonliving things.

© Harcourt

How Do Living Things Grow and Change?

1 Build Background

Access Prior Knowledge

When to Use	Proficiency Levels
Before introducing the lesson 🕐 20 minutes	✔ Beginning ✔ Intermediate Advanced

Give students an opportunity to name living things and make a list on the board. Add humans to the list and remind students that people are living things. Point out that they were babies once. Encourage them to use sentences to tell ways their bodies have changed since then and how they will change in the future. Ask students to choose other living things on the list and discuss what they know about how those things change and grow over time.

Preteach Lesson Vocabulary

> **life cycle, metamorphosis, inherit**

List the vocabulary words on the board.

- Have students look through pages 40–44 to find the vocabulary words. Help students pronounce them.
- Have students recall the discussion of how humans change during their lifetimes. Explain that those changes make up the *life cycle*. Discuss the meaning of each term in the phrase and have students use those definitions to explain what they think a life cycle might be.
- Explain that one kind of life cycle is *metamorphosis*. Metamorphosis occurs when the adult organism looks very different from the baby—like a butterfly and a caterpillar.
- Ask students to describe ways they look like their moms or dads. Point out that although dogs come in many shapes and sizes, puppies almost always look a lot like their parents. Explain that this happens because the puppies *inherit* features from their parents.

Build Fluency

Have students echo read these sentences using a cadence that emphasizes the phrase *life cycle*. Encourage them to write their own examples and teach them to the group.

- Babies go through a life cycle to become adult humans.
- Puppies go through a life cycle to become adult dogs.
- Calves go through a life cycle to become adult cows.

② Scaffold the Content

When to Use With pp. 38–45 🕐 20 minutes	Proficiency Levels ✔ Beginning ✔ Intermediate ✔ Advanced

Preview the Lesson

- Ask students to point to the title on page 38 as you read it aloud. Explain that they will discuss this question in the lesson. Have students observe the picture. Read the caption and use it as a starting point for a discussion about how plants grow.
- Have students scan the pictures of the life cycles of plants and animals on pages 40–43. Remind students that plants are living things. Discuss with students how plants grow and change. Compare these changes to the life cycles of animals.
- Have students preview the pictures on page 44 to make educated guesses at some characteristics animals inherit from their parents.

Investigate, p. 39

Materials: paper towel, seed, zip-top bags, index cards

- Before students begin the Investigate, help them preview or review the names of some items in the Materials list. Point out each object and say the name.
- Have students write *paper towel*, *seed*, and *bag* on separate index cards, then match each label to the appropriate object. Students can work in pairs and alternate roles so that one student scrambles the objects/cards and then the other student sorts them.
- Demonstrate the difference between wet and dry paper towels. Say the adjective clearly as you show each type and write the terms on the board.

Modify Instruction—Multilevel Strategies

Background/Experience The concept of the development of living things, the focus of this lesson, involves understanding that living things grow and change over time. Learners will better understand this concept when relating it to actual plants and animals in their surroundings. The following exercises provide opportunities for students to see how plants and animals grow and change.

Beginning Ask students to make simple drawings of the life cycle of a plant, using a different index card for each stage. They can use page 40 for reference. Partners can shuffle and trade cards, then put them in order. Partners should discuss why they put the cards in the order that they did.

Intermediate Ask students to make simple drawings of the life cycle of an animal, using a different index card for each stage. They can use page 42 for reference. Have them use simple words to summarize how the animal changes over time.

© Harcourt

Advanced Ask students to make simple drawings of the stages of metamorphosis, using a different index card for each stage. They can use page 43 for reference. Have students write a few sentences summarizing the changes.

For All Students Have students make a small poster with their drawings and present the work to a group or to the class. Have them summarize the changes shown in the drawing.

Extend

Have the students complete the Show What You Know activity on page 11 to demonstrate their understanding of the life cycles of plants and animals.

③ Apply and Assess

How Does It Grow?

When to Use	Proficiency Levels
With Reading Review p. 45	✔ Beginning
	✔ Intermediate
🕐 20 minutes	✔ Advanced

Materials: paper, markers, colored pencils, or crayons

- Divide students into three groups. Assign each group one of the following topics: *bean plant, dog,* or *butterfly.*
- Have students write the name of their organism at the top of a piece of paper. Direct them to draw the steps in the life cycle of that organism and number the stages.
- Display the three drawings. Discuss with all of the students how the life cycles are alike and different. Summarize the similarities and differences by writing them on chart paper and display the list with the posters.

Informal Assessment

Beginning	Intermediate	Advanced
Show a picture of a seed. Ask students to name or draw a picture of the adult form of a seed. *(Students should name or draw a plant or tree.)*	Have students order a set of cards with drawings of the stages of an animal's life cycle. Ask them to explain their answer. *(Students should be able to order the cards correctly.)*	Have students summarize in words the life cycle of any plant or animal. *(Answers will vary.)*

Name _____

Date _____

Growing and Changing

Draw a picture to show each stage of the life cycle of a bean plant. Repeat for a butterfly.

Bean Plant

Step 1:	Step 2:	Step 3:	Step 4:

Butterfly

Step 1:	Step 2:	Step 3:	Step 4:

© Harcourt

 School-Home Connection: Have students take this page home to share with family members. They can use this page to tell about the life cycles of plants and animals.

2 Types of Plants

Develop Scientific Concepts and Vocabulary

In this chapter, students will learn about some of the many types of plants, and how scientists distinguish between them. They will also learn what a plant needs to live and grow well. In addition, students will explore how plants are able to make their own food through the process of photosynthesis.

Preview Scientific Principles

Walk through the chapter with students, pausing to read aloud or to have volunteers read aloud the three questions that are lesson titles. Encourage students to briefly discuss each question and to tell what they already know that might help them to answer the questions.

When to Use With Chapter Opener	Proficiency Levels
25 minutes	✔ Beginning ✔ Intermediate ✔ Advanced

Lesson 1: What Do Plants Need to Live?

- Have students share where they have seen plants. For each example that students mention, discuss the area in which the plant was growing, what the plant was sitting in, how much light it received, and whether it was watered by a person or received water from rain.
- Ask students if they have ever seen a plant growing in a dark, dry place.

Lesson 2: What Are Some Types of Plants?

- Take students for a walk around the school building. Point out the plants, including trees, as you go. Invite students to notice the leaves, flowers, and any visible seeds on the plants.
- Encourage students to use descriptive words to compare the trees they see.

Lesson 3: How Do Plants Make Food?

- Review the basic needs of most living things—air, water, energy, and a place to live.
- Ask students to tell some of the foods they eat. Point out that they must use resources they find or buy to get the needed energy from food.
- Have students consider how plants get the food that they need.

© Harcourt

Practice

Make a concept web to help students recall what they already know about plants. Write *PLANTS* in the center of a piece of butcher paper. Have students give examples of plants, words that describe how plants look, and any information about what plants need to grow. When students have completed the web, talk about what suggestions fit with each of the categories listed above. Display the concept web and encourage students to add to it as they read the chapter.

Apply

Write the story from the following chart on the board and have students take turns echoing or reading a line aloud and pantomiming each of Mr. Green's actions. Have students copy each sentence onto a separate piece of paper. Have them illustrate each page and bind them into a book. Invite students to reread the story with a partner.

Mr. Green's Garden

Mr. Green enjoys growing plants. He grows plants from seeds. He plants them where there is lots of sun and he gives them lots of water. The plants grow strong and healthy. Some of Mr. Green's plants are flowers. He cuts them and puts them in a vase. Some of his plants are vegetables. He picks them, washes them, and puts them in a salad. Mr. Green has a very large tree growing near his garden. He sits under it as he looks at his flowers and eats his salad.

What Do Plants Need to Live?

① Build Background

Access Prior Knowledge

When to Use	Proficiency Levels
Before introducing the lesson 15 minutes	✔ Beginning ✔ Intermediate Advanced

Materials: plant

Show students a plant. Have them look at the plant, touch it, and dig into the soil to see what lies beneath. Encourage them to discuss their observations. Say *plant* as students repeat the word aloud. Invite them to name any plant parts that they know.

Preteach Lesson Vocabulary

roots, nutrients, stem, leaf

Materials: plant

List the vocabulary words on the board.

Have students find each vocabulary word in the lesson.

- Display a plant for students to see. Point out the *stem* and a *leaf* as you name them. Have students echo the words.
- Dig away some of the soil to expose the roots. Say *roots* as you point to this plant part. Have students echo the word.
- Ask students if they know why the plant sits in the soil. Explain that the soil has *nutrients* in it that are taken in by the roots. Plants use nutrients to help them grow and stay healthy. We get nutrients from the foods that we eat. Nutrients help us to grow, too.

Build Fluency

Have students work with a partner to tell the parts of a plant using the following sentence frame:

The plant has _____.

You may wish to provide a plant or labeled picture of a plant to help them remember.

© Harcourt

② Scaffold the Content

Preview the Lesson

- Read together the title of the lesson. Tell students that they will find the answer to this question in the lesson.
- Read the caption on page 56. Relate the needs of a plant to the needs of the students.
- Have students discuss all the places they see plants growing. If possible, take students on a walk around the schoolyard, pointing out the parts of some of these plants.
- Identify the pictured plant parts on page 59 as you read the captions.
- As students view the plants on page 60, ask them to discuss how these plants look different from the others they have seen in the lesson.

Investigate, p. 55

Before students begin the Investigate:

- Give each student cups filled with sand, potting soil, and gravel. Invite them to touch each material. Write the names of each material on index cards and use the cards to label each substance.
- Discuss with students what a *healthy* plant would look like. Point to plant parts as you note that in a healthy plant, the leaves are green and full and the stem is firm.

Modify Instruction—Multilevel Strategies

Materials: watering can, a cup of soil, picture of the sun

Comprehensible Input Point to each item as you review that water, soil, and sunlight are needed by plants to live. Remind students that plants also need air, but unlike us, they use carbon dioxide in air, not oxygen. Use these items and the following activities to help students understand the basic needs of a plant and the way in which those needs are met.

Beginning Tell students that a plant needs sunlight. Have them point to the representative item on the table that meets this need. Then ask them to point to the item that meets a plant's need for nutrients. Finally, ask students to point to the item that keeps a plant from becoming dried out.

© Harcourt

Intermediate Tell students that you have a plant, but that it is not growing well. Explain that the plant is in a cup of sand. Have them tell which plant need is not being met. Next, tell them that your plant is wilting. Ask which need of the plant is not being met. Finally, tell students that your plant is in a closet. Again, ask which need is not being met.

Advanced Use the same examples provided in the intermediate activity. Have students write advice for how to better care for the needs of your plant.

For All Students Help students to see how the parts of the plant are specially suited to help it meet its needs.

Extend

Have students complete the Show What You Know activity on page 17 to show their understanding of plant needs and how those needs are met.

③ Apply and Assess

Make a Needs of Plants Mobile

When to Use With Reading Review p. 61 ⏱ 20 minutes	Proficiency Levels ✔ Beginning ✔ Intermediate ✔ Advanced

Materials: clothes hanger, yarn, card stock, markers, magazines, scissors, glue

- Invite students to draw or find a picture of a healthy plant. Have them glue the picture on a piece of card stock and tie this image to the middle of their clothes hanger.
- Have students draw or find images to represent the four basic needs of plants. Again, have them glue these images to card stock. Attach these pictures with longer pieces of yarn so that they hang lower than the plant.
- Display the mobiles. Invite students to tell a partner what a plant needs to grow and to stay healthy. Have them discuss how their mobiles show those needs.

Informal Assessment

Beginning	Intermediate	Advanced
Ask students to draw a picture showing two of the things that a plant needs to live. *(Answers: Students should draw a picture indicating any two of the following: soil, water, sunlight, or air.)*	Have students finish this sentence frame: *Four things a plant needs are _____, _____, _____, and _____.* *(Answers: water, soil, air, and light)*	Read this scenario. *A plant is not growing. It is in a cup of rocks and sand. The roots are dry, and the leaves are yellow. The plant is in a dark corner.* Have students advise the plant's owner, telling how to care for it. *(Answers should include placing the plant in soil, giving it water, putting it in a sunny spot.)*

© Harcourt

Name _____

Date _____

What a Plant Needs

Finish each sentence by drawing what a plant needs. On the back of this paper, write directions for how to care for a plant.

A plant needs

A plant needs

A plant needs

A plant needs

School-Home Connection: Have students take this page home to share with family members. They can use it to tell about a plant's needs and how those needs are met.

© Harcourt

What Are Some Types of Plants?

① Build Background

Access Prior Knowledge

When to Use	Proficiency Levels
Before introducing the lesson 20 minutes	✔ Beginning ✔ Intermediate Advanced

Materials: pictures of a deciduous and an evergreen tree, pine needles, a broadleaf

- Display both pictures. Have students tell how the two trees look different.
- If possible, show an example of needles from a pine tree and a broadleaf from a deciduous tree. Have students examine both samples. Help them describe each of the leaves using sensory words.

Preteach Lesson Vocabulary

> **seed, deciduous, evergreen**

Materials: seeds of various types, pictures of deciduous trees in summer and in winter, pictures of evergreen trees in summer and in winter

List the vocabulary words on the board.

- Tell students that *seeds* are parts of plants that can grow and develop into new plants. Provide a variety of seeds for students to sort and examine. Include seeds from fruits and vegetables, flower seeds, and seeds from different kinds of trees.
- Show students a picture of a deciduous tree in summer. Point out the leaves on the tree. Then show students a picture of a similar tree in winter. Tell students that a tree that loses its leaves in winter is called a *deciduous* tree. Have students repeat this word after you.
- Show students an evergreen tree both in summer and in winter. Point out that the tree looks the same in both seasons. Tell students that this tree loses its leaves, which are called needles, but not all at one time. Explain that this is called an *evergreen* tree.

Build Fluency

Review with students the difference between deciduous and evergreen trees. Then have them work with a partner to look at plants around the school. Invite them to use the following sentences to correctly describe each tree they see.

This tree is deciduous.

This tree is an evergreen.

© Harcourt

② Scaffold the Content

Preview the Lesson

When to Use With pp. 62–70	Proficiency Levels
20 minutes	✔ Beginning ✔ Intermediate ✔ Advanced

Materials: leaf, seed, flower

- Have students find the title of the lesson on page 62. Tell students that they will find the answer to this question in the lesson.
- Show students a leaf, a seed, and a flower. Name each for students. Invite students to look at the pictures and captions on pages 64–70 and to identify these plant parts.
- On pages 66 and 67, work with students to brainstorm descriptive words for each type of leaf. Invite students to repeat each descriptor while pointing out the leaf.
- Walk students through the remaining images of the lesson.

Investigate, p. 63

Before students begin the Investigate:

- Review the language in the Investigate to help students understand the directions for each step of the activity.
- Show students that *to split* means "to break in half." Then point out the hand lens and name it for students.
- Tell students that *to moisten* means "to make damp." In this case, students will moisten one paper towel but not use too much water. Point to the wet towel and say *wet*. Do the same for *dry*.
- If needed, work with students to find words to describe their results.

Modify Instruction—Multilevel Strategies

Language and Experience Write the words *deciduous* and *evergreen* on the board. Tell students that the word *deciduous* comes from the Latin word *decidere*, which means "to fall down or off." Help students to connect the word origin to the fact that *deciduous* describes a kind of tree whose leaves fall down or off at the same time each year. Then underline the word *evergreen*. Tell students that this is a compound word. Draw a line between *ever* and *green*. Explain the meaning of *ever* as "always." Help students to see that an *evergreen* tree is a kind of tree that always stays green. Its leaves do not fall off all at once.

Beginning Provide several pictures of deciduous and evergreen trees. Have students make two groups of pictures, one for each type of tree. Then point to each group and name it as students repeat each word.

© Harcourt

Intermediate Discuss with students how deciduous and evergreen trees look different in the winter season. Have students use this sentence frame to compare the way the trees look in this season: *In winter, deciduous trees* _____, *but evergreens* _____.

Advanced Explain to students that scientists classify trees by grouping them as deciduous or evergreen trees. Have students make a two-column chart and record how the two types of trees are alike and different. Invite them to also record how the two types of trees make seeds and if they have flowers.

For All Students Help students classify the pictures of trees in the lesson into groups.

Extend

Have students complete the Show What You Know activity on page 21 to demonstrate their understanding of deciduous and evergreen trees.

③ Apply and Assess

Make a Tree Chart

When to Use With Reading Review p. 71	Proficiency Levels
20 minutes	✔ Beginning ✔ Intermediate ✔ Advanced

Materials: poster board, old nature magazines, glue, markers

- Have students fold a large piece of poster board in half lengthwise. Write the words *deciduous* and *evergreen* on the board. Have students copy each tree type onto the poster board.
- Students may look through old nature magazines and find and cut out pictures of each type of tree. They may then glue them in the appropriate columns of the chart.
- Have students tell a partner why they sorted the pictures the way they did.

Informal Assessment

Beginning	Intermediate	Advanced
Show students pictures of deciduous and evergreen trees. Ask students to point to a *deciduous* tree and repeat the word after you. Do the same for *evergreen*. (Answer: Students should accurately identify the types of trees and repeat each term.)	Have students complete the following sentence frames: A(n) _____ tree loses its leaves each fall. A(n) _____ tree only loses leaves from time to time. (Answer: deciduous; evergreen)	Remind students that deciduous trees do not make food in the winter, but that evergreen trees make food all year long. Have students write sentences to explain why this is so. (Possible answer: Deciduous trees have no leaves in winter to make food. Evergreen trees do, so they continue to make food in winter.)

Name _____

Date _____

Trees Through the Seasons

On the top part of the page, draw a deciduous tree in summer and in winter. On the bottom part of the page, draw an evergreen tree in summer and in winter. On the back of the paper, write a sentence telling the difference between the two types of trees.

Deciduous Tree

Summer	Winter

Evergreen Tree

Summer	Winter

School-Home Connection: Have students take this page home to share with family members. They can use this page to tell about deciduous and evergreen trees.

© Harcourt

How Do Plants Make Food?

① Build Background

Access Prior Knowledge

When to Use	Proficiency Levels
Before introducing the lesson 20 minutes	✔ Beginning ✔ Intermediate Advanced

Materials: green plant

- Ask students what they eat when they are hungry. Discuss how the food they eat gives them more energy and helps them to grow.

- Show students a plant. Ask them how a plant gets food for energy. Tell them that a plant uses water, sunlight, and carbon dioxide in the air to make its own food.

- Discuss the differences between the way a plant gets food and the way people do.

Preteach Lesson Vocabulary

photosynthesis, chlorophyll

Materials: green plant, paper

List the vocabulary words on the board.

- Write the words *photosynthesis* and *chlorophyll* on the board. Read each word and clap the syllables. Have students follow along.

- Remind students that a plant makes its own food. Tell them that the way a plant makes food is by a process called *photosynthesis*.

- Direct attention to the plant. Ask a volunteer to tell the plant's color. Explain that the plant is green because it contains a substance called *chlorophyll*. Give students a green leaf and have them rub the leaf on some paper. They should be able to see the green substance on the paper. Explain that plants need chlorophyll to use the energy from sunlight to make food.

Build Fluency

Review with students that we eat many different kinds of plants. Have them work with a partner to name plants they eat. Invite them to use the following sentence frame:

I eat _____.

© Harcourt

② Scaffold the Content

Preview the Lesson

- Remind students that all living things need energy to live, grow, and be healthy.

- Have students look at the images on pages 74 and 75. Point to each component described on page 75 as you read the captions. Review with students that the stem of a plant carries water to its leaves. Connect the fact that the plant then uses this water, along with carbon dioxide, sunlight, and chlorophyll, to make its food.

- Have students discuss ways they know that plants can help them and harm them. Then read the captions on page 76. Ask students who may have had experiences with the harmful plants mentioned here to share their experiences.

Investigate, p. 73

Before students begin the Investigate:

- Read the title and help students to see why it might relate to a plant making food.

- Relate this activity to the Investigate that students completed in Lesson 1. Review what makes a plant *healthy*. Show students a healthy plant as you point out the green leaves, the strong stem, and flowers.

- After students complete the Investigate, help them verbalize the differences between the two plants.

Modify Instruction—Multilevel Strategies

Language and Vocabulary

- Begin by writing the word *photosynthesis* on the board. Underline the beginning part of this word, *photo-*. Explain that this prefix means "light." Help students to see that *photosynthesis* is the process whereby a plant uses light to make food.

- Then write *chlorophyll* on the board. Tell students that the word part *chloro-* comes from a Greek word meaning "green." The second part of the word, *-phyll*, comes from a Greek word meaning "leaf." *Chlorophyll* is a green pigment that makes leaves green.

Beginning Write the words *chlorophyll* and *photosynthesis* on the board. Ask students to circle the word that means "the process a plant uses to make food." Have them underline the word that means "a green color in plants."

© Harcourt

Intermediate Have students answer the following questions: *Is photosynthesis the way a plant makes food? What color is chlorophyll? Does photosynthesis use light? What part of the word tells you this?*

Advanced Have students define each word in a complete sentence.

For All Students Help students to understand the role that chlorophyll plays in photosynthesis, and how both are important to a plant.

Extend

Have students complete the **Show What You Know** activity on page 25 to demonstrate their understanding of a healthy plant and one that is not healthy.

③ Apply and Assess

Draw a Plant

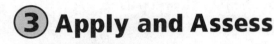

When to Use With Reading Review p. 77 ⏱ 20 minutes	Proficiency Levels ✔ Beginning ✔ Intermediate ✔ Advanced

Materials: drawing paper, markers

- Have students draw a picture of a healthy plant and label its parts.
- Invite them to draw and label all the elements necessary for the plant to complete photosynthesis *(sunlight, carbon dioxide, water, and chlorophyll).*
- Have students share their pictures with the group. Invite them to tell how the plant uses the elements in the picture to make food.

Informal Assessment

Beginning	Intermediate	Advanced
Write *chlorophyll* and *photosynthesis* on index cards. Have students point to the word that means "a green color in plants." Then have them repeat the word after you. Ask students to point to the word that means "the way a plant makes food." Again, have students repeat the word. *(Answers: chlorophyll; photosynthesis)*	Have students copy and complete the following sentence frames: The green color in a plant is called _____. It helps the plant use _____ to make food in a process called _____. *(Answers: chlorophyll; sunlight; photosynthesis)*	Have students make a list of the things a plant needs to make food. Then have them give a brief explanation of photosynthesis. *(Answer: Students should list carbon dioxide, water, chlorophyll, and sunlight. They should also be able to explain that a plant takes in water, carbon dioxide, and sunlight. The chlorophyll in the leaves uses the energy from sunlight to make sugar.)*

Needs of Healthy Plants

In the first box, draw a picture of a healthy plant. In the second box, draw a
picture of a plant that is not healthy. On the back of this page, write what
a plant needs to stay healthy.

Healthy Plant	**Unhealthy Plant**

School-Home Connection: Have students take this page home to share with
family members. They can use this page to tell about what keeps a plant healthy.

3 Types of Animals

Develop Scientific Concepts and Vocabulary

In this chapter, students will learn that all animals have certain basic needs. Students will learn that animals can be classified into two categories: vertebrates and invertebrates.

Preview Scientific Principles

Walk through the chapter with students, pausing to read aloud or have volunteers read aloud the three questions that are lesson titles. Encourage students to briefly discuss each question and to tell what they already know that might help them answer the questions.

When to Use With Chapter Opener	Proficiency Levels
🕐 30 minutes	✔ Beginning ✔ Intermediate ✔ Advanced

Lesson 1: What Do Animals Need to Live?

- With students, brainstorm a list of animals. Write them on the board. Be sure to include animals that will appear in this chapter, such as: *clam*, *crocodile*, *duck*, *spider*, and *worm*.

- Talk about the needs of various animals on the list. Ask, for example, "Where does a toucan live? Do you know what crabs eat?" Summarize the discussion by saying, "All animals have basic needs. No matter where they live, animals need air, water, and food."

Lesson 2: What Are Vertebrates?

- Stand with your back to the students. With your hand, reach back and trace the length of your spine, saying, "This is my backbone." Have students do the same.

- Tell students that some animals have a backbone, but others do not. A bear has a backbone, for example, but a worm doesn't.

- Animals with a backbone are called *vertebrates*, and animals that don't have a backbone are called *invertebrates*.

- Have small groups each create a list of all the animals on the board that are vertebrates. Then have them share their lists.

© Harcourt

Lesson 3: What Are Invertebrates?

- Write *correct* and *incorrect* on the board. Point out that the prefix *in-* changes the meaning of *correct* from "right" to "wrong."
- Write *vertebrate* and *invertebrate* on the board. Ask, "If vertebrates are animals with a backbone, what are invertebrates?" (animals with no backbone)
- Have small groups each create a list of invertebrates. (Students can refer to the list on the board.) Then have them share their lists. Reconcile any errors.

Practice

To help students practice using key vocabulary, play the following guessing game. On index cards, write the names of animals from the class lists. Give one of these cards to each student. Tell students to pretend that they are the animal written on their cards. Then, have students circulate around the classroom asking each other these three questions: "Are you a vertebrate or an invertebrate? Where do you live? What do you eat?" After receiving the answers to these three questions, each student guesses what animal the other is. Students whose identity is correctly guessed sit down. The game continues in this way until all the animals are guessed.

Apply

Write the following poem on the board, and lead students in several choral readings. To create innovations on the poem, erase the words *bear* and *snails*. Have students replace these animals with the names of a vertebrate and invertebrate, respectively.

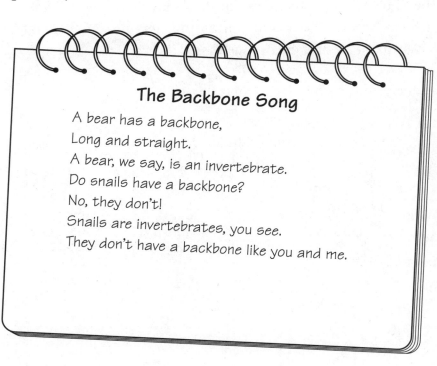

The Backbone Song

A bear has a backbone,
Long and straight.
A bear, we say, is an invertebrate.
Do snails have a backbone?
No, they don't!
Snails are invertebrates, you see.
They don't have a backbone like you and me.

Lesson 1 — What Do Animals Need to Live?

① Build Background

Access Prior Knowledge

When to Use	Proficiency Levels
Before introducing the lesson 25 minutes	✔ Beginning ✔ Intermediate Advanced

Ask students "What do you need to live?" Write student responses on the board. Review each item on the list, and help students distinguish between items that might be wants, as opposed to needs. Erase those items that are not really essential to survival. In the end, you should have the following items on the list: *food, air, water,* and a *place to live.* Tell students that animals need the same things that we need.

Preteach Lesson Vocabulary

> **oxygen, shelter**

List the vocabulary words on the board.

Use the following definitions and strategies to support comprehension:

- *Oxygen is the air we breathe.* Take a deep breath of air to help illustrate. Invite students to inhale deeply and then to slowly exhale as they say the word *oxygen.*

- *Shelter is a place to live.* On the board, draw a picture of a cave and a house. Say, "A cave is shelter for a bear. A house is shelter for people." Flip through pages 86–93 and help students identify the different animal homes that are shown in the photos. Teach the names of the following habitats: *dam, nest, lodge,* and *burrow.* Invite students to pantomime an animal "coming home" to each of these habitats, and encourage them to verbalize a descriptive sentence as they do so.

Build Fluency

Write the following poem on the board, underlining the words *bird, nest, whale,* and *sea.*

The <u>bird</u> lives in the <u>nest</u>,
The <u>whale</u> lives in the <u>sea</u>,
But home's the very nicest place
For a little child like me.

© Harcourt

② Scaffold the Content

Preview the Lesson

When to Use With pp. 86–92	Proficiency Levels
⏱ 15 minutes	✔ Beginning ✔ Intermediate ✔ Advanced

- Direct students to page 86. Write the title on the board: *What Do Animals Need to Live?* Have the class read the question chorally. Then, direct them to page 89. Have a volunteer read the subtitle aloud, and write it on the board. Ask students to predict the next subtitle. Have them check on page 90. Write it on the board. Repeat this procedure.

- Preview the photos in this lesson. Teach or review the names of all the animals and habitats shown. Ask intermediate and advanced students to provide this vocabulary by asking, for example, "What animal do you see on page 86?" Have beginning students echo their responses.

Investigate, p. 87

Before the students begin the Investigate, have them play a matching game using word cards with the names of animals and their homes.

- On separate index cards, write two sets of the following words: *bird, nest, bear, den, beaver, lodge, rabbit,* and *burrow.* Make sure that students understand the meaning of these words.

- Form two teams. Shuffle the cards and place them on a tabletop in the form of a grid.

- Players on the teams take turns turning over two cards to see if they have a match.

Modify Instruction—Multilevel Strategies

Language and Vocabulary

- Verbal constructions with the verb *get* can be difficult for English language learners, because they involve prepositions. Write these examples on the board:

  Spiders get oxygen through tiny holes.

  An elephant gets food with its trunk.

- Sometimes the preposition is followed by another verb. That verb is usually conjugated in the gerund form. Write these examples on the board:

  Whales get oxygen by rising to the surface.

  A giraffe gets leaves by stretching its neck.

© Harcourt

Beginning Have these students repeat after you as you recite the sentences on the board.

Intermediate Prompt students by giving them the names of different animals. Have them create new sentences based on the sentence patterns on the board. If you give them the prompt *Ants*, for example, they should be able to say *Ants get oxygen through tiny holes*.

Advanced Have these students write sentences of their own creation based on the sentence patterns on the board. Invite students to share their work with the class.

For All Students Ask students to look for sentences with the verb *get* in the lesson.

Extend

Have the students complete the **Show What You Know** activity on page 31. They can take the word cards home to play the matching game with their families.

③ Apply and Assess

Make Animal Cartoons

When to Use With Reading Review p. 93 🕐 30 minutes	Proficiency Levels ✔ Beginning ✔ Intermediate ✔ Advanced

Materials: crayons, paper

- Have students draw an animal of their choice.
- Demonstrate how to draw a large speech balloon over the animal's head.
- Encourage students to write a sentence that the animal might say. The animal should say something about its habitat or diet. Provide an example.
- Have students present their work in front of the class.

Informal Assessment

Beginning	Intermediate	Advanced
Ask students to draw and label pictures of three animals that they learned about in this lesson. *(Answers will vary.)*	Ask students to draw and label pictures of three animals that they learned about in this lesson. Have students write a sentence about where the animal lives. *(Answers will vary.)*	Ask students to write three sentences about an animal of their choice. Students should tell: 1) Where it lives; 2) What it eats; 3) How it gets food and/or water. *(Answers will vary.)*

© Harcourt

Name _____

Date _____

Matching Animals

1. Cut out the word cards.

2. Draw a picture for each word.

3. Use the cards to play a matching game. Match the animals with their habitats.

bird	nest
bear	den
beaver	lodge
rabbit	burrow

School-Home Connection: Have students take this page home to share with family members. They can play the matching game at home.

What Are Vertebrates?

① Build Background

Access Prior Knowledge

When to Use	Proficiency Levels
Before introducing the lesson ⏱ 25 minutes	✔ Beginning ✔ Intermediate Advanced

- Review the word *backbone*. First, stand with your back to the class and, reaching behind your back, trace the length of your spine, saying, *This is my backbone.* Encourage students to do the same. Review the vocabulary for other body parts.

- Have students practice using short responses with *yes* and *no* by asking questions such as: *Does a whale have legs? Does it have eyes?* Model correct responses: *No, it doesn't. Yes, it does.* Invite volunteers to pose similar questions.

Preteach Lesson Vocabulary

> **vertebrate, mammal, bird, reptile**

List the vocabulary words on the board.

Review the word *vertebrate*, reminding students that a vertebrate is an animal with a backbone. Ask students to help you brainstorm a list of vertebrates. Use vocabulary cards, photos, and simple sketches to support acquisition of new vocabulary. Then, tell students to help you classify the names of all the animals into one of the following categories: mammals, birds, reptiles, amphibians, fish.

Build Fluency

Write the following rhyme on the board. Lead students in a choral chant.

Frogs, penguins, kangaroo, kangaroo;
Frogs, penguins, kangaroo, kangaroo.
Cats and dogs and monkeys, too.
Frogs, penguins, kangaroo, kangaroo.

② Scaffold the Content

Preview the Lesson

 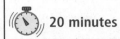
With students, flip through pages 94–102. Pause to look at the photos, asking students to name the animals shown in each. After previewing page 98, ask students to supply the names of other mammals that they know besides the ones shown (kangaroo, tigers, and pigs). In the same way, pause after each section and ask students to provide the names of animals besides the ones shown in the photos that belong to the same category.

Investigate, p. 95

Before the students begin Investigate, introduce students to the physical characteristics that are associated with mammals and other animals.

- Using a photo of a seal, sea lion, polar bear, or walrus, point to the rolls of fat on the animal. Tell students: *This is fat. It is also called blubber. The fat, or blubber, keeps the animal warm in winter.*

- Point out the animal's fur. If necessary, show a photo of a different animal, such as a bear or lion. Explain that animals often lose fur in the hot summer months.

- Using other photos or word cards, teach the names of other animal body parts.

Modify Instruction—Multilevel Strategies

Comprehensible Input Distribute drawing paper and crayons or pencils. Tell students that you are going to draw a picture of an eagle on the board. As you begin drawing, indicate to students that they are to follow along by drawing their own pictures of an eagle. Verbalize as you draw to create comprehensible input for students; say, for example: *I'm going to start with the head. This is the crown of the eagle's head. It has white feathers on top. The eagle has a very sharp beak. Now I'm going to draw the eagle's body. It has big wings and a tail. Don't forget to draw the eagle's talons.* When you are finished, label each body part.

Beginning Students copy labels on their drawings. Circulate as they work and make sure that their drawings are properly labeled.

Intermediate When students are finished with their drawings, ask them to talk about the eagle and its body parts. Model how to do this with your picture on the board. Point to each body part as you say: *This is the eagle's beak. These are its wings,* and so on.

Advanced Encourage students to write a sentence about eagles, based on their drawings.

For All Students Ask students to look through the photos in this lesson to find other animals with legs, wings, beaks, and feathers.

Extend

Have the students complete the Show What You Know activity on page 35. Encourage students to draw pictures illustrating their sentences on the back of the paper.

③ Apply and Assess

Make a Book about Vertebrates

When to Use	Proficiency Levels
With Reading Review p. 103 ⏱ 20 minutes	✔ Beginning ✔ Intermediate ✔ Advanced

Materials: paper, colored pencils or crayons

- Form pairs or small groups of students.
  Have students work together to draw a picture of a vertebrate that they have learned about in this lesson. Tell them to draw one of the following: mammal, bird, reptile, amphibian, or fish.
- Tell students to write captions in the pattern, *A polar bear is a mammal.*
- Guide students in making a cover with a title, such as *A Book of Vertebrates.*
- Help students staple their pictures together to create a book.

Informal Assessment

Beginning	Intermediate	Advanced
Ask students to draw and label pictures of three verte-brates that they learned about in this lesson. *(Answers will vary.)*	Ask students to draw and label pictures of three vertebrates that they learned about in this lesson. In addition, have students write a sentence that tells about the animal's physical traits. *(Answers will vary.)*	Ask students to write two or three sentences about a vertebrate of their choice. Students should tell what category the animal belongs to (mammal, bird, reptile, amphibian, or fish), and name some of its physical characteristics. *(Answers will vary.)*

Name _____

Date _____

Describing Animals

1. Read the name of each animal.

2. Check off the body parts that the animal has.

3. Write a sentence about the animal. Follow the example.

	Eagle	Polar bear	Goldfish	Tiger	Penguin	Whale
Fur						
Feathers	X					
Wings	X					
Legs	X					
Beak	X					
Scales						
Gills						

1. An eagle has feathers, wings, legs, and a beak. _____

2. _____

3. _____

4. _____

5. _____

6. _____

 School-Home Connection: Have students take this page home to share with family members. They can read their sentences aloud for family members.

© Harcourt

What Are Invertebrates?

① Build Background

Access Prior Knowledge

When to Use	Proficiency Levels
Before introducing the lesson ⏱ **25 minutes**	✔ Beginning ✔ Intermediate Advanced

On the board, label simple drawings of the following animals: *butterfly, spider, snail.* Ask students what these three animals have in common. If necessary, ask students to think of it this way: "What's something that all three of them don't have?" Through a process of elimination, guide students to the conclusion that they don't have a backbone.

Preteach Lesson Vocabulary

invertebrate

Write the vocabulary word on the board.

Draw students' attention once again to the drawings you made.

- Label the names of the following body parts: *wings, legs, shell.* Ask students to think of other invertebrates that have wings, legs, and shells. Remind students that certain animals, such as birds, may have wings but they also have a backbone, so they are not classified as invertebrates.

- Point out that the snail's body has two main parts: a soft body and an outer shell. We say that it has a *simple* body. The spider and butterfly, however, have more than two body parts that are connected together. We say that they have *complex* bodies.

- Draw a line through the middle of the butterfly. Point out that the left side is the same as the right side. This means that the butterfly is *symmetrical.*

Build Fluency

Here is an adaptation of a traditional rhyme featuring the bumblebee.

Over in the meadow in a hive in the sun
An old bumblebee and her babies had fun.
"Let's buzz!" said the mother to her three little ones.
And they buzzed and were happy in the hive in the sun.

© Harcourt

② Scaffold the Content

When to Use With pp. 104–112	Proficiency Levels
⏱ 35 minutes	✔ Beginning ✔ Intermediate ✔ Advanced

Preview the Lesson

Have students look at the lesson title on page 104. Ask a volunteer to read it aloud: *What Are Invertebrates?* Invite students to guess the names of the animals that they are going to learn about in this lesson. Write student responses on the board. Then, flip through the pages of the lesson with students, reading the subtitles and previewing the photos. As you do so, check off the animal names on the board that appear in the text and captions. Use the photos to teach or review the words *insect*, *spider*, *tick*, *snail*, *clam*, *squid*, and *worm*.

Investigate, p. 105

Before the students begin Investigate, use live earthworms to review the word *worm*.

Place one of the worms on a flat surface. Have students gather to observe the worm. Ask: *Does the worm have legs? How does it move?* Point out that the worm contracts its muscles in a wave. With your finger, follow a wave-like movement through the worm's body to support comprehension. Ask students to think of another animal that moves in the same way. They may mention slugs or snails, for example.

Modify Instruction—Multilevel Strategies

Language and Vocabulary The names of many invertebrates are compounds. These compounds may at first seem long and unwieldy to English language learners. Help students see the constituent parts of the following compounds: *bumblebee, butterfly, dragonfly, earthworm, firefly, honeybee, jellyfish, ladybug, starfish.*

Beginning Have students copy these words from the board and draw a line between the two parts of each compound.

Intermediate Have students write "math problems" for each of these compounds in the following pattern: *bumble + bee = bumblebee.*

Advanced Have students write a sentence for three of the compounds in the list.

For All Students Ask students to look for these compounds as they go through the lesson. You can even turn this activity into a "scavenger hunt" and give points to teams for each word that they find. Have teams copy the whole sentence in which the compound appears. The team that finds the most compounds in the shortest period of time wins.

Have the students complete the **Show What You Know** activity on page 39.

③ Apply and Assess

Make Butterfly Cards

When to Use With Reading Review p. 113 ⏱ 30 minutes	Proficiency Levels ✔ Beginning ✔ Intermediate ✔ Advanced

Materials: white construction paper, tempera, scissors, pipe cleaners

- Demonstrate how to fold the sheet in half and cut out the shape of a butterfly wing from the folded corner. When the paper is unfolded, there will be a perfectly symmetrical shape of a butterfly.

- Have students apply paint to one or both of the wings. Tell them to fold and press the wings together while the paint is still wet. Have them wait a few moments and then unfold the wings. The paint will leave a symmetrical design on both sides.

- To represent the butterfly's body, guide students in gluing a pipe cleaner to the center of the butterfly so that the tip of the cleaner peeks out above the edge of the card.

Informal Assessment

Beginning	Intermediate	Advanced
Ask students to draw and label three different animals that they learned about in this lesson. (Answers will vary.)	Ask students to draw and label three different animals that they learned about in this lesson. Have students write a sentence about each animal. (Answers will vary.)	Ask students to choose an animal that they learned about in this lesson. Have them draw a picture of that animal and then write three sentences about it, telling what they learned. (Answers will vary.)

Making Invertebrates

1. Read the word parts.

2. Cross out the word that does not fit.

3. Write the new word. Follow the example.

bumble	~~worm~~	bee

bumblebee _____

dragon	fly	bug

_____

earth	worm	fish

_____

fire	crab	fly

_____

honey	dog	bee

_____

jelly	fish	spider

_____

lady	bug	squid

_____

star	horse	fish

_____

 School-Home Connection: Have students take this page home to share with family members. They can read aloud each word for family members. Encourage students to draw a picture of each animal.

Chapter 4
Where Living Things Are Found

Develop Scientific Concepts and Vocabulary

In this chapter, students will learn what an ecosystem is and will explore different types of ecosystems. Students will learn some ways that living things adapt to changes in their environment. Students will also learn how ecosystems change over time.

Preview Scientific Principles

Walk through the chapter with students, pausing to read aloud or to have volunteers read aloud the four questions that are lesson titles. Encourage students to briefly discuss each question and to tell what they already know that might help them answer the questions.

When to Use With Chapter Opener	Proficiency Levels
⏱ 20 minutes	✔ Beginning ✔ Intermediate ✔ Advanced

Lesson 1: What Are Ecosystems?

- Write the word *system* on the board and have students say the word with you. Define system as "a group of things that form a whole."
- Put *eco* and *system* together to show the word *ecosystem*. Explain that an *ecosystem* has to do with the living and nonliving things in an environment and how they relate to, or interact with, each other.

Lesson 2: What Are Some Types of Ecosystems?

- Share pictures of different ecosystems, such as desert, grassland, forest, ocean, and fresh water ecosystems. Help students identify each kind by name.
- Call out different characteristics (i.e. wet, dry) and have students point to the ecosystem that corresponds to the characteristics you name.

Lesson 3: How Do Living Things Survive in Ecosystems?

- Explain that an *instinct* is not learned, but is something you are born knowing. Instincts help animals survive. Ask students to think of ways animals survive or protect themselves.
- Ask students what they do to *adapt* to changes in weather. Then share a picture of an animal *hibernating* or animals *migrating* when the weather becomes cold.

© Harcourt

Lesson 4: How Do Ecosystems Change?

- Have students predict how an ecosystem might change if there were a flood or fire.
- Have students think of positive and negative ways people change ecosystems.

Practice

Direction students' attention to the chapter opener and read aloud the information about Everglades National Park. Explain that the Everglades is a *protected area* (people are not allowed to build there). Invite students to name animals they know and guess the ecosystems in which these animals live. Have students think of the characteristics of each ecosystem that suits each animal or of the ways the animals seem to have adjusted to life in the particular ecosystem. You may wish to provide pictures of animals for students to match to ecosystems.

Apply

Write the following on the board or on large poster paper. Have students take turns echoing each animal and ecosystem. Call on volunteers to draw lines from the animal to the ecosystem they *think* it lives in. They'll read the chapter to verify their responses.

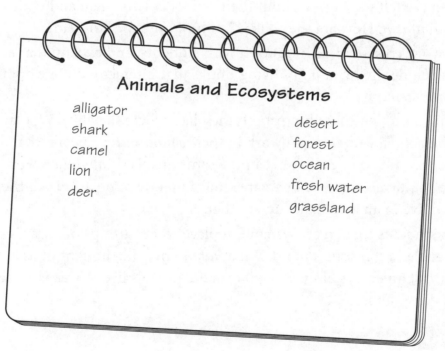

Animals and Ecosystems

alligator	
shark	desert
camel	forest
lion	ocean
deer	fresh water
	grassland

What Are Ecosystems?

① Build Background

Access Prior Knowledge

When to Use	Proficiency Levels
Before introducing the lesson 15 minutes	✔ Beginning ✔ Intermediate ✔ Advanced

Materials: pictures of a city, suburb, and rural area

Hold up pictures of a city, suburb, and rural area and ask students to point to the kind of place in which they live. Have students tell what they need to live (i.e., food, water, air, space). Ask volunteers to name animals or plants that live in deserts, jungles, oceans, and so on. Ask what animals need to live in the places where they live.

Preteach Lesson Vocabulary

> environment, ecosystem, population, community, habitat

List the vocabulary words on the board.

- Have students look through the lesson to find the vocabulary words.
- Ask students to tell something about their school *environment* and their home *environment*. How are they alike, and how are they different?
- Write the word *ecosystem*, pronounce it with students, and explain that an *ecosystem* includes living and nonliving things that interact with one another in an *environment*.
- Ask a volunteer to tell something about the place where they live. Who are some of the people who live and work in their *community*? Explain that a group of the same beings that live in the same area is a *population*. For example, all squirrels that live in an area make up one population. All the people who live in an area make up another.
- Explain to students that an ecosystem is a place where groups of organisms interact, such as a forest or a pond. But a *habitat* may be thought of as a smaller part of an ecosystem where plants and animals live. A tree is a habitat in a forest ecosystem.

Build Fluency

Assign each group a particular ecosystem, such as a desert, a forest, and an ocean. Have each group talk about their assigned ecosystem and describe it, using lesson vocabulary words, to help distinguish their ecosystem from another group's. Have groups share and compare facts about their ecosystems.

② Scaffold the Content

Preview the Lesson

- Ask students to point to the lesson title as you read it aloud. Explain that they will find the answer to this question in the lesson.

- Direct attention to the photo as you read aloud the Fast Fact. Invite students to look through the chapter to see other environments and the living things found in each.

- Continue to look through the chapter with students. Help them understand that different types of organisms make up an *ecosystem*; that an *ecosystem* is the living and nonliving things in an *environment* that interact; and that all the *populations* that live in an *ecosystem* form a *community*.

Investigate, p. 125

Before students begin the Investigate:

- Write the headings *Living* and *Nonliving* on the board and elicit examples of things that belong in each category. For example, plants and animals belong under *Living*; air, water, soil, and rocks belong under *Nonliving*. Ask for one difference between living and nonliving things (i.e., living things grow and nonliving things do not).

- Work with the class to set up their observation tables. Then have students work in small groups to complete the Investigate. Encourage students to share their findings and conclusions.

Modify Instruction—Multilevel Strategies

Background/Experience Help students understand the kinds of living and nonliving things that can be found in an environment. Remind students that the kinds of living and nonliving things may differ in different environments. Walk around the school and have students point to and identify some of the living and nonliving things they see in the environment. Call on volunteers to tell about environments they may know about in other countries. What similarities and differences do students note?

Beginning Have students select an environment and draw or copy what it looks like, including plants and animals. Have students write or copy words that identify things in their drawing. Have them practice saying words or sentences that tell about their drawings.

© Harcourt

ESL Support 43

Intermediate Prepare a word web graphic organizer for students to copy. In the center, have students write the name of an ecosystem, such as desert, forest, or ocean. Once students have chosen an ecosystem, have them brainstorm the names of plants and animals that live in it. Help students spell the names of plants and animals they choose.

Advanced Have students design their own graphic organizers to show the organisms that live and interact in particular ecosystems.

For All Students Have students compare two different ecosystems in terms of temperature, precipitation, or other characteristics.

Extend

Have students complete the **Show What You Know** activity on page 45 to demonstrate their understanding of a pond ecosystem.

③ Apply and Assess

Make Yourself At Home

When to Use	Proficiency Levels
With Reading Review p. 131	✔ Beginning
	✔ Intermediate
⏱ 20 minutes	✔ Advanced

Materials: pictures of animals, plants, and names of environments written on index cards

- Explain that the idiom *make yourself at home* means "make yourself comfortable." Have students look through the pages of the chapter and point to and name the plants and animals that are "comfortable" in each environment pictured.

- Call on volunteers to come to the front of the room. Give each student a plant, an animal, or an environment card. Tell other students that they are to "match" the animals and plants to the environments in which they belong.

- Call on seated students to name two students that "belong together." In some cases, there may be more than two students who match, such as when more than one organism belongs in the same environment.

Informal Assessment

Beginning	Intermediate	Advanced
Have students look outside the window, through the pages of their textbooks, or through nature magazines to find and name organisms they have read about. Whenever possible, have students identify the members of an ecosystem that interact. *(Answers will vary.)*	Have students draw or complete a graphic organizer that represents a particular ecosystem. Then have students write or complete simple sentences that relate to their graphic organizer. For example, A cactus grows in the _____ (*desert*). *(Answers will vary.)*	Ask students to choose one ecosystem and write a paragraph about it. Include the living and nonliving things that interact with one another. *(Answers will vary.)*

Name _____

Date _____

A Pond Ecosystem

This word box lists some living and nonliving things of a pond ecosystem. Classify them as living things and nonliving things in the boxes below. On the back of the page, draw a pond ecosystem.

fish	rocks	water	snail	heron
turtle	cattails	water lily	air	insect
frog				

Living Things	Nonliving Things

School-Home Connection: Have students take this page home to show family members what they have learned about a pond ecosystem.

© Harcourt

2 What Are Some Types of Ecosystems?

① Build Background

Access Prior Knowledge

When to Use	Proficiency Levels
Before introducing the lesson	✔ Beginning
🕐 15 minutes	✔ Intermediate
	✔ Advanced

- Write the words *animals* and *plants* on the board and have students brainstorm examples of each as you record them on the board.

- Point to different animal and plant names and ask students to tell where each organism lives. Write these examples of ecosystems (desert, ocean, forest, and so on) on the board.

- Have students brainstorm words that come to mind as you point to and say aloud the name of each ecosystem. Review words such as *hot*, *cold*, *wet*, *dry*, and so on.

Preteach Lesson Vocabulary

> **desert, grassland, forest**

List the vocabulary words on the board.

- Have students look through the lesson to find the vocabulary words. Have students say the name of each ecosystem aloud.

- Direct students' attention to photographs in the lesson that are examples of each ecosystem. Have students discuss things they see in each photograph.

- Ask simple questions based on information that may be supported in the photos. For example, "What is a desert like? How did the ecosystem *grassland* get its name? Why is this ecosystem called a *saltwater* ecosystem? Do you think freshwater fish would do well in the ocean? What does the ocean contain that is not in fresh water streams and ponds? What is the plant life of a forest like?"

Build Fluency

Once again, direct students' attention to the photographs of the various ecosystems in the text. In round-robin fashion, have students point to something in a photo and say something about it. If they are able, encourage students to speak in whole sentences.

© Harcourt

② Scaffold the Content

Preview the Lesson

- Have students point to the lesson title as you read it aloud. Explain to students that they will find the answer to this question in the lesson.

- Read aloud the Fast Fact. Have students discuss the picture.

- Read aloud the captions in the chapter as students study the photos. Point out that Earth has different kinds of land ecosystems and different kinds of water ecosystems. Tell students that most of Earth is made up of saltwater ecosystems.

Investigate, p. 133

Before students begin the Investigate:

- Read aloud the title *Grass Roots* and discuss its double meaning. Point out that a "grass roots" effort is one that starts "at the bottom" with everyday people. An example of a grass roots effort to stop land pollution might be students collecting recyclables.

- Point out the word *blade* in step 2. This word has several meanings. Here, *blade* refers to a leaf of grass.

- Have students work in small groups. After the Investigate, ask students to discuss how the roots of a grass plant would compare with the roots of a tree.

Modify Instruction—Multilevel Strategies

Comprehensible Input As students review material from the chapter, help them understand the ways in which ecosystems differ from one another (i.e., temperature and rainfall). Use the photos in the text to highlight important differences between ecosystems. Ask students to consider what would happen to the animals in an ecosystem if they were threatened by pollution, such as an oil spill. Do they think that animals would be able to adjust to a new ecosystem? Why, or why not? What are some examples of significant differences between ecosystems?

Beginning Have students use colored pencils or markers to illustrate different ecosystems. Suggest that they label some of the things in their drawings and be prepared to say something about what they have drawn.

Intermediate Have students illustrate an ecosystem of their choice and write a sentence or two that tells something about that ecosystem.

Advanced Have students select one ecosystem to write about. In a paragraph, have them tell about their ecosystem and identify some kinds of organisms that live there.

For All Students Have students compare two ecosystems in terms of temperature, rainfall, and location on Earth.

Extend

Have students complete the **Show What You Know** activity on page 49 to demonstrate their understanding of ecosystems.

③ Apply and Assess

Home Sweet Home

When to Use	Proficiency Levels
With Reading Review p. 139 🕐 20 minutes	✔ Beginning ✔ Intermediate ✔ Advanced

Share the meaning of the idiom *home sweet home*. Then have students work with partners to choose one organism from one particular ecosystem. Together, they may write sentences that tell something about both the organism and its ecosystem without revealing the name of the organism. (Consider pairing less able students with more fluent students to ensure a level of conversation necessary for collaboration.) Call on volunteers to share what they have written. See if the class can infer the organism from the clues provided about the organism and its ecosystem.

Informal Assessment

Beginning	Intermediate	Advanced
Write specific ecosystems on the board (forest, desert, ocean, fresh water, and so on) or tape pictures of them on the board. Have students work individually or with partners to list words that relate to each ecosystem. After they have finished, call on students to note words on their lists that are opposite in meaning, such as *wet* and *dry*. *(Answers will vary.)*	Show students pictured examples of different ecosystems and have them write one or two sentences about each ecosystem. *(Answers will vary.)*	Have students choose two ecosystems and write a paragraph comparing them. *(Answers will vary.)*

© Harcourt

Name _____

Date _____

Who Lives Where?

Write the name of each animal or plant in the box in the correct ecosystem below.

deer	cactus	trout	shark

Desert	Forest
Fresh Water	**Salt Water**

School-Home Connection: Have students take this page home to help them explain some of Earth's different ecosystems.

© Harcourt

Lesson 3

How Do Living Things Survive in Ecosystems?

① Build Background

Access Prior Knowledge

When to Use	Proficiency Levels
Before introducing the lesson 15 minutes	✔ Beginning ✔ Intermediate ✔ Advanced

Place a small potted plant on a windowsill and water it. After a few days, students will notice that all the leaves face the window. Turn the pot around so that the leaves face inside. Wait a few days. What happens? Ask students how this *adaptation* helps plants to survive. Have students consider ways in which they themselves *adapt* to seasonal changes *(wear heavy clothes in cold weather; move indoors during a storm)*. Ask students to think of things animals do to survive.

Preteach Lesson Vocabulary

adaptation, instinct, hibernate, migrate, camouflage, mimicry

List the vocabulary words on the board. Have students locate the vocabulary words in the lesson.

- Have students say each word several times with you, clapping out each syllable they hear. Find a visual example in the text that helps to illustrate the word's meaning.

- Whenever possible, relate the vocabulary words to students' own experiences. For example, ask students, "What is one thing you do to *adapt* to changes in weather? What do you *instinctively* do when you touch something hot? How does a costume or disguise 'cover up' or *camouflage* a person?"

Build Fluency

Have students say the vocabulary words that end in *-tion* (*hibernation, migration, adaptation*), noting in each case the syllable that gets the accent. Write the words on the board and have students pronounce each word as you point to it. Then write the words *adapt*, *migrate*, and *hibernate* on the board. Point out that these words are *verbs*, or action words. Ask students what geese do when they *migrate* and what an animal does when it *hibernates*.

© Harcourt

② Scaffold the Content

Preview the Lesson

- Ask students to point to the lesson title as you read it aloud. Read the caption for the picture so that students understand how beavers survive in their environment.
- Continue to look through the pictures and captions for the lesson with students. Help them understand that adaptations, whether physical or behavioral, help animals survive.

Investigate, p. 141

Before students begin the Investigate:

- Read aloud the title and discuss that the word *hide* in this context means "to keep out of sight." Explain other meanings of the word *hide*. Examples include "The child tried to *hide* (keep secret) his fear" and "Leather shoes are made from *hide* (skin of an animal)."
- Have students study the photos in the Investigate that show how an insect can hide in its environment.
- Have students work in groups as you read aloud the steps of the Procedure.
- Ask students why insects may need to hide. Ask for other examples of animals that hide themselves through the use of color.

Modify Instruction—Multilevel Strategies

Language and Vocabulary Explain that a verb is a word that describes an action, such as sit, stand, jump, or smile. Remind students that the words *adapt*, *migrate*, and *hibernate* are verbs that may be changed to nouns when *-tion* is added. The *-tion* ending always signals a noun. Write the verb *mimic* and explain that *mimic* means "to imitate." For example, "Some parrots *mimic* people's voices." Then add the letters *ry* to *mimic* and explain that you've just formed the noun *mimicry*, which means "the practice of mimicking." The following activities provide opportunities for students to reinforce parts of speech and common word endings.

Beginning Prepare a list of words and a list of suffixes. Have students match a word with a word ending to make a new word. For example, *help + ful*; *friend + ly*; *new + ness*. Have students practice using the words in sentences, such as "I can *help* you. I can be very *helpful*."

Intermediate Prepare a list of verbs and have students change each verb to another part of speech by adding or taking away letters. For example, *create (creation)*, *migrate (migration)*, *hand (handy)*, *light (lightness)*, *empty (emptiness)*.

Advanced Have students complete the Intermediate exercise. Then have them write a sentence for each of the words in the pairs of words.

For All Students Play the game "Presto Chango" by turning verbs into nouns. Prepare a list of verbs for students to change into nouns. For example, *survive* becomes *survival*.

Extend

Have students complete the Show What You Know activity on page 53 to demonstrate their understanding of the ways living things survive in ecosystems.

③ Apply and Assess

Word Families

When to Use With Reading Review p. 147 ⏱ 20 minutes	Proficiency Levels ✔ Beginning ✔ Intermediate ✔ Advanced

- Students form teams. Each team writes lists of words that are related. Examples could include verb-to-noun changes as discussed earlier. They also should include words that share similar meanings though different spellings. For example, *speak* and *speech*, *fly* and *flight*.
- Encourage students to explain why they think their word choices are related. This exercise should prove helpful in understanding some of the spelling irregularities of the English language.

Informal Assessment

Beginning	Intermediate	Advanced
Review with students that animals have *instincts* for staying alive. Instincts are ways of acting or behaving that an animal is born with and doesn't have to learn. Have students draw an example that shows animal instinct (a bird building a nest; a beaver building a dam; an animal hibernating; geese migrating). *(Answers will vary.)*	Ask students to complete the following sentence frames with the appropriate words: A bird is born knowing how to build a _____ *(nest)*; All beavers know how to _____ *(build dams)*; When geese _____, *(migrate)* they travel back and forth to a certain place. *(Answers will reflect an understanding of animal instincts that help them survive.)*	Review with students the fact that animal adaptations involve both physical traits, such as fur changing color in the seasons, as well as behavioral traits, such as hibernation. Have students write a paragraph about an example of one animal adaptation and how that adaptation helps the animal to survive. *(Answers will vary.)*

Name _____

Date _____

Staying Alive

Animals are born with adaptations that help them to survive in their environment. For each box, draw an animal that is born with the adaptation listed in the box. On the line below each box, write the name of the animal you drew.

Camouflage	Mimicry

_____   _____

Hibernation	Migration

_____   _____

School-Home Connection: Have students take this page home to family members to share their understanding of animal adaptations.

© Harcourt

ESL Support 53

How Do Ecosystems Change?

① Build Background

Access Prior Knowledge

When to Use	Proficiency Levels
Before introducing the lesson 15 minutes	✔ Beginning ✔ Intermediate ✔ Advanced

Materials: "before" and "after" pictures, such as a wooded area and a housing development in that area

Have students imagine what happens to a forest when people start to build houses or roads there. Ask students to think of natural events that cause changes in an ecosystem *(fires, floods, droughts)*. Sometimes the changes to an environment, whether caused by people or nature, cause animals to leave an area.

Preteach Lesson Vocabulary

> resource

Write the vocabulary word on the board.

- Write the word *resource* on the board and have students practice saying the word with you. Explain that a *resource* is something that is found in nature and not made by people. Resources are used by organisms. Ask students to name examples of resources, such as trees, water, coal, minerals, soil, and air.

- Ask students to name examples of things that can affect or destroy natural resources, such as fire, pollution, drought, lightning, and flooding.

- Review the word *ecosystem* with students and ask them to think of things that cause changes in an ecosystem.

Build Fluency

Have students look out the window or take a walk outside of school to identify natural resources. Have students say and write the names of natural resources they see. Then have them make a list of products made by people, such as buildings or roads. Back in class, have students talk about the products made by people and which natural resources are used to make those products.

② Scaffold the Content

Preview the Lesson

- Ask students to point to the lesson title as you read it aloud. Also read aloud the caption about Hoover Dam. Ask students to imagine how building the dam changed the ecosystem of the area around the dam.

- Look through the lesson with students, giving them the chance to look at the pictures, captions, and subheads. Guide them to understand that ecosystems change over time, whether caused by nature or by people; that these changes can be short-term or long lasting; and that people and animals can find ways to share the same ecosystems.

Investigate, p. 149

Before students begin the Investigate:

- Tell students that this activity will help them understand cause-and-effect relationships. An example of cause and effect is when a stream flows differently *as a result of* a beaver's dam. Ask students to name other cause-and-effect relationships.

- Point out that the sand represents Earth, the leaves and twigs represent plants and trees, and the water represents a river or stream.

- Ask students to work in small groups as you read aloud and guide them through the steps of the Procedure.

Modify Instruction—Multilevel Strategies

Background/Experience Have students think of one ecosystem, such as a pond or a forest. Then have them imagine that ecosystem being hit by a great flood. What changes would result? Have students draw two pictures of their ecosystem showing "before" and " after" versions.

Beginning Have students identify pictures in their books that illustrate ways that ecosystems can change. Have them find an example of a natural cause of change and a change caused by people.

Intermediate Have students use words to describe the cause-and-effect relationships illustrated by the volcanic eruption sequence and by the aerial photographs of the forest and lake area before and after its development by people.

Advanced Have students write a paragraph explaining some causes of change to ecosystems.

For All Students Call on volunteers to suggest ways that people change ecosystems in positive ways, such as by planting trees and by protecting organisms.

Extend

Have students complete the **Show What You Know** activity on page 57 to demonstrate their understanding of natural resources and the ways we may protect them.

③ Apply and Assess

Helping the Environment

When to Use	Proficiency Levels
With Reading Review p. 153	✔ Beginning
🕐 20 minutes	✔ Intermediate
	✔ Advanced

Materials: paper cups, soil, flower seeds, water

- Divide the class into groups and provide each group with its own materials.

- Have students fill their paper cups halfway with soil and then poke a small hole in the soil. Have students drop two flower seeds into the hole, cover it with a thin layer of soil, and add just enough water to moisten the soil.

- Place students' cups in a sunny window. Have students check their cups daily, adding water only when the soil becomes dry.

- Have students clean up a sunny area around the school and prepare it for planting.

- When the seedlings are about 3 inches tall, plant the seedlings.

- Ask students to tell how this activity helps the environment.

Informal Assessment

Beginning	Intermediate	Advanced
Have students open their books and point to examples of changes that are harmful to ecosystems. Have them also point to examples that affect an ecosystem for the better. *(Answers will vary but should demonstrate an understanding of positive and negative effects to an ecosystem.)*	Ask students to make two drawings that illustrate how an ecosystem can change—one positively and one negatively. Have them write the *cause* for each change. Have them write one *effect*, or result, of the change. *(Answers will vary but should demonstrate an understanding of the cause-and-effect relationships.)*	Have students write a paragraph describing a change that is harmful to an ecosystem. Then have them write a second paragraph describing a change to an ecosystem that is positive. Instruct students to identify the cause and effect for each ecosystem change. *(Answers will vary.)*

© Harcourt

Name _____

Date _____

Protecting Natural Resources

Choose a natural resource from the word box, or think of one of your own.
Write the resource below. Then draw a picture to show one thing people can
do to protect this natural resource.

air	water	trees or other plants
land	rocks	

School-Home Connection: Have students take this page home to family
members to share their understanding of natural resources and ways we can
protect them.

© Harcourt

5 Living Things Depend on One Another

Develop Scientific Concepts and Vocabulary

In this chapter, students will learn that all living things play an important role, either as producers, consumers, or decomposers. Consumers can be further divided into herbivores, carnivores, or omnivores. Students will see how these different groups of living things interact, and how together they form intricate and interdependent food webs.

Preview Scientific Principles

Walk through the chapter with students, pausing to read aloud or to have volunteers read aloud the three questions that are lesson titles. Encourage students to briefly discuss each question and to tell what they already know that might help them answer the questions.

When to Use With Chapter Opener	Proficiency Levels
⏱ 25 minutes	✔ Beginning ✔ Intermediate ✔ Advanced

Lesson 1: How Do Plants and Animals Interact?

- Ask students what they need in order to grow and be healthy. Help them to see that food gives them the energy they need to grow.
- Similarly, ask what animals need to grow and be healthy. Again, point out that food gives animals energy to grow and be healthy.
- Ask students what things a plant needs to grow and be healthy. Explain that a plant needs sunlight, water, and nutrients in soil to make its own food.

Lesson 2: What are Food Chains?

- Show students a paper chain made up of circles. Have students examine each circle. Discuss that each circle is an individual part, but when linked together the parts create a chain. Each piece of the chain is important because it connects it to the next.

Lesson 3: What are Food Webs?

- Have students stand in a circle. Give one student a ball of string. Have that person hold an end of the string and then toss the ball to someone else.
- Invite the next student to hold the string and pass the ball to someone else. Continue this until each person has some of the string to hold.

© Harcourt

- Have students observe that each of them is connected by the string. Point out the web pattern that has emerged as the string was passed from person to person. Then, choose one person to drop his or her piece of string. Invite students to discuss the result.

Practice

Help students to begin thinking about the ways that living things depend on one another by creating a concept map. In the center of the map, write *How Living Things Depend on One Another*. Then guide students by asking questions, such as, *What things do you need? Who or what helps you get those things?* Lead students to think about how people help them but also to consider what plants and animals they need. Record their answers.

Then, have each student choose one element from the map and draw a picture illustrating that idea. Have students write captions for their pictures to share with the class.

Apply

Write the following poem on the board, and have students take turns echoing or reading a line aloud. Then give students grocery store advertisements from local newspapers. Invite them to search for pictures of these foods or other foods that they like to eat. Have them cut out the images and use them to create a collage of food they eat. Finally, have students write a sentence identifying one kind of food they eat that gives them energy to grow.

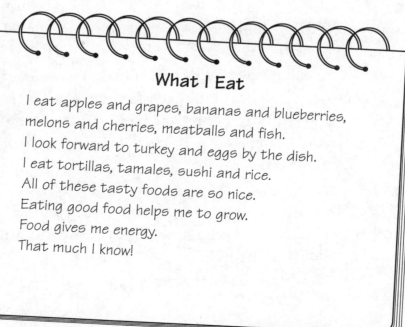

What I Eat

I eat apples and grapes, bananas and blueberries,
melons and cherries, meatballs and fish.
I look forward to turkey and eggs by the dish.
I eat tortillas, tamales, sushi and rice.
All of these tasty foods are so nice.
Eating good food helps me to grow.
Food gives me energy.
That much I know!

Lesson 1

How Do Plants and Animals Interact?

① Build Background

Access Prior Knowledge

When to Use	Proficiency Levels
Before introducing the lesson 20 minutes	✔ Beginning ✔ Intermediate ✔ Advanced

Ask students if any of them has ever grown or cared for a plant. Discuss the things that plants need to live. Point out that we do not feed plants things like bread, cheese, or meat. Instead, plants are able to make their own food from sunlight, water, and nutrients in the soil. Explain that even though people and plants get their food in different ways, both need food to make energy to grow and be healthy.

Preteach Lesson Vocabulary

> **producer, consumer, decomposer, herbivore, carnivore, omnivore**

List the vocabulary words on the board.

Have students look through the lesson to find the vocabulary words.

- Make a simple, three-box flowchart on the board. Write *producer, consumer,* and *decomposer,* in that order in the boxes. Point out that a *producer* is a living thing that makes its own food. Draw a simple picture of a plant in this box. A *consumer,* however, cannot make food. It eats other things for food. Draw a picture of an animal in this box. Point to the box for *decomposer.* Explain that this kind of living thing breaks down dead things to use for food. Draw a picture of a worm in this box.

- Explain that there are three different kinds of consumers. Draw three lines from the consumer box. Create a box at the end of each line. Label the boxes *herbivore, carnivore,* and *omnivore* respectively, and explain what each term means. Have students name examples of each kind of consumer. Write examples of each kind in the boxes.

Build Fluency

Have students work with a partner and echo the following sentences. Students may extend the activity by adding examples of each type of food.

Herbivores eat plants. (Extension example: *Herbivores eat plants like grass.*)

Carnivores eat meat.

Omnivores eat plants and meat.

© Harcourt

② Scaffold the Content

Preview the Lesson

When to Use With pp. 162–168	Proficiency Levels
🕐 25 minutes	✔ Beginning ✔ Intermediate ✔ Advanced

- Ask students to point to the title of the lesson and have them read it aloud with you.

- Read the section title on page 165. Have students point to each word as you read it aloud. Then read the captions for each picture. Point to the sunflower, and say *producer*. Point to the bird, and say *consumer*. Point to the earthworm, and say *decomposer*.

- Review the remaining pictures of the lesson with students, and read the captions aloud. Tell them that in this lesson they will learn that living things may be classified as *herbivores*, *carnivores*, and *omnivores*.

Investigate, p. 163

Before students begin the Investigate:

- Display the animal picture cards, one at a time, and have students name the animals. For animals that may be unfamiliar, supply their names and have students echo them.

- Point out that the word *table* has more than one meaning. In step 1, *table* means "chart."

- Brainstorm with students words that might be used to describe the shapes of teeth in step 4. As students name the words, write them on the board and draw a picture of what shape that tooth might look like. Some words students might mention are *pointy*, *sharp*, *wide*, *narrow*, *flat*, *long*, and *short*.

Modify Instruction—Multilevel Strategies

Language and Vocabulary Help students to see that the vocabulary words in this lesson can be understood by looking more closely at their word parts. Write the words *herbivore*, *carnivore*, and *omnivore* on the board. Draw a line between the first part of each word and the *-vore* ending. Define the first part of each word: *herbi-* relates to a kind of plant called an *herb*; *carni-* relates to the bodies of animals that we call *meat*; and the word part *omni-* means "many," or "all." The suffix *-vore* means "one that eats." Help students put the meaning of the word parts together to see that each word describes what a certain group of living things eats.

Beginning Write each word on a card. Display the cards, one at a time. Cover the *-vore* ending, and say the first word part. Have students echo. Then cover the first part of the word and say *-vore*, as students echo. Display the whole word. Run your finger under the entire word as you say it aloud. Have students follow the same procedure.

© Harcourt

Intermediate Show students each word card. Have them say the word aloud. Then, invite them to use what they learned about the word's parts to tell a definition of each word.

Advanced Have students write each word without using the word cards. Then invite them to check their spelling against the correct spelling on the cards. Finally, ask students to write a definition for each word.

For All Students Help students to expand their understanding of each category of *consumer* by exploring what animals eat in each group.

Extend

Have students complete the **Show What You Know** activity on page 63 to demonstrate their understanding of the different kinds of teeth that animals have.

③ Apply and Assess

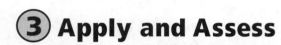

Make a Chart of Consumers

When to Use	Proficiency Levels
With Reading Review p. 169 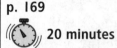 20 minutes	✔ Beginning ✔ Intermediate ✔ Advanced

Materials: chart paper, nature magazines, scissors, tape

- Draw three columns on chart paper and display the chart on a wall or bulletin board. Label the columns *herbivore, carnivore,* and *omnivore,* respectively.

- Have students cut out a variety of pictures of consumers from old nature magazines. Then, help them to sort the pictures into the correct category shown on the chart. You may need to use the Internet or other resources to identify the diets of some animals.

- Invite each student to name the animal and its category as they tape it in the correct column of the chart.

Informal Assessment

Beginning	Intermediate	Advanced
Show students cards with the words *herbivore, carnivore,* and *omnivore.* Also provide one picture of an animal in each category. Point to a category and say it. Have students repeat the category name. Ask students to match the animal with its correct category. Repeat for each category. *(Answer: Students should correctly match each animal with its category.)*	Using the same word cards, have students match each animal to its appropriate category. Then have students use complete sentences to tell which animal belongs to which category. *(Answer: Students should be able to correctly match each animal to its appropriate category and relate the information in a complete sentence.)*	Have students use the pictures and category names to write sentences telling which animals belong to which category. Then have them write an additional sentence for each category that explains what belonging to the specific group means in terms of the animal's diet. *(Answers will vary. Possible answer: Cows are herbivores. Cows only eat plants.)*

© Harcourt

Name _____

Date _____

Tooth Shape

In Box 1, draw a tooth of an animal that eats only plants. In Box 2, draw the tooth of an animal that eats only other animals. On the back, write the names of animals that have these kinds of teeth.

Box 1	Box 2

School-Home Connection: Have students take this page home to share with family members. They can use this page to discuss what tooth shape tells about what animals eat.

© Harcourt

What Are Food Chains?

① Build Background

Access Prior Knowledge

When to Use	Proficiency Levels
Before introducing the lesson 20 minutes	✔ Beginning ✔ Intermediate ✔ Advanced

Invite students to share what they had to eat for dinner the night before. Write the responses on the board. Read through the items on the list, identifying food items that come from plants as well as from animals. Help students to see that most of us eat a variety of food items that come from both plants and animals. Remind students that living things, or organisms, get their energy from the food they eat.

Preteach Lesson Vocabulary

food chain, energy pyramid, predator, prey

List the vocabulary words on the board.

Have students look through the lesson to find the vocabulary words.

- Invite volunteers to come to the front of the room and link hands one by one. Explain that the students form a chain and are connected together. Explain that a *food chain* shows how living things are connected by the ways they get energy from food.

- Display a model of a pyramid. Point out that the base of the pyramid is much larger than the top. Tell students that an *energy pyramid* is a diagram that shows visually how energy gets used in a food chain. Draw an example on the board. Explain that as energy is passed up through the pyramid, most of the available energy has been used by the living things in the previous level. Since less energy is passed to the next higher level, there are fewer living things as you move up the pyramid.

- Relate the terms *predator* and *prey* with the acts of hunting and being hunted. Explain that the predator is an animal that hunts another animal called the prey.

Build Fluency

Have students work with a partner to find and relate examples of animals featured in the lesson and what they eat. Students may use the following sentence frame:

_____ eat(s) _____.

Example: *Birds eat grasshoppers.*

© Harcourt

② Scaffold the Content

When to Use	Proficiency Levels
With pp. 170–176 20 minutes	✔ Beginning ✔ Intermediate ✔ Advanced

Preview the Lesson

- Have students follow along as you read the lesson title.

- Look together at the images on pages 172 and 173. Read the captions aloud, and have students move their finger in order as the images relate the order of the food chain.

- Have students count the number of living things shown at each level of the energy pyramid on page 175. Ask why there are fewer organisms as they move up the pyramid.

- Have students discuss the way each of the animals on page 176 might catch his prey. Read the captions and note that size and speed play a role in hunting.

Investigate, p. 171

- For students who need help, point out where the *bottom right-hand corner* of an index card is.

- For students who are not familiar with the animal names mentioned in step 2, provide pictures of each living thing for them to copy. Or you might display word cards with each image for students to copy onto their own index cards.

- Tell students that a *model* is something you make that represents something. A model helps you to see information that you might not otherwise see. Provide examples, such as a model of the solar system or a model of a cell.

Modify Instruction—Multilevel Strategies

Background/Experience The concept of a food chain involves an understanding of sequential order and how one event leads to the next. The following exercises provide opportunities for students to practice ordering events and understanding ways to relate the order of events.

Beginning Show students cards with pictures of grass, a grasshopper, a lizard, and an owl. Have students put the cards in the correct order to show how the animals get energy.

Intermediate Show students the same set of cards. Ask questions related to the order in the food chain, such as, "Who eats the grass?" "What is the first level of this food chain?" "What does the owl eat?" Have students point to and name the appropriate card.

Advanced Have students order the cards to show the correct sequence of this food chain. Then have students write a paragraph explaining the food chain. Encourage them to use words that indicate sequence, such as *first, then, next,* and *finally.*

For All Students Help students to see the relationship between a food chain and an energy pyramid. Explain that with each level of the food pyramid, the amount of energy is less because the living things of the previous level have used much of the available energy for living and growing.

Extend

Have students complete the **Show What You Know** activity on page 67 to demonstrate their understanding of a food chain.

③ Apply and Assess

Make a Linked Food Chain

When to Use With Reading Review p. 177 🕐 30 minutes	Proficiency Levels ✔ Beginning ✔ Intermediate ✔ Advanced

Materials: card stock, markers, yarn, hole punch

- Invite students to work with a partner. Have the pairs choose one food chain described in the lesson.
- On separate pieces of card stock, have them draw pictures of each organism of the chain.
- Assist students in punching holes in each card stock. Using the yarn, help students link the cards together in the correct order. Display the chains around the classroom.
- Invite students to name in order the organisms that make up the food chain.

Informal Assessment

Beginning	Intermediate	Advanced
Use pages 172 and 173. Have students point to and name the correct order of the organisms in this food chain. (*Answer: grass, grasshopper, lizard, owl*)	Have students complete the following sentence frame: A food chain always begins with a _____. (*Answer: producer*)	Have students create a graphic organizer that shows the order of the food chain shown on pages 172 and 173. Then, using sequence words, have them write a paragraph describing the food chain. (*Answers will vary.*)

Name _____

Date _____

A Food Chain

Write or draw the order of organisms in the food chain. On the back, write a sentence telling which organism is the producer. Write a second sentence telling which organisms are the consumers.

caterpillar	fox	bird	leaf

School-Home Connection: Have students take this page home to share with family members. They can use their pictures to tell about food chains.

ESL Support   67

© Harcourt

What Are Food Webs?

① Build Background

Access Prior Knowledge

When to Use	Proficiency Levels
Before introducing the lesson ((🕐)) 15 minutes	✔ Beginning ✔ Intermediate Advanced

Ask students to name their favorite food. Write their responses on the board. Then ask them if this is the only food they eat. Guide students to see that most animals eat more than one kind of food. Ask students to think about how many different food chains they are part of, given all the different kinds of foods they like to eat.

Preteach Lesson Vocabulary

food web

Write the vocabulary words on the board.

- Point out the word *web* in the term *food web*. Ask if students have seen this word before. Some students may mention a spider web. If possible, show students a picture of a spider web. Have them notice how the strands of silk in a web reach out in many directions and overlap in some places.

- Explain that a food web is a visual way to show how many food chains can overlap. Remind students of the fact that they eat more than one kind of food and belong to more than one food chain.

Build Fluency

Have students think about all the different food chains to which they belong as they consider all the different kinds of food they eat. Working with a partner, have them use the following sentence frame to build fluency:

I eat _____. I also eat _____.

Examples: *I eat hamburgers. I also eat apples.*

② Scaffold the Content

Preview the Lesson

When to Use With pp. 178–184 🕐 20 minutes	Proficiency Levels
	✔ Beginning
	✔ Intermediate
	✔ Advanced

- Read the title aloud as students track the print with their fingers.
- Have students find the term *food web* in the lesson. Help them to read the words around the highlighted term to find the definition. Then, have students look at the food web in the picture. Have students point to each animal as you read what it eats. Help students to see how all the animals are connected in the web.
- Read together the captions on pages 182 and 183, and have students retell in their own words how these animals defend themselves against predators.
- Guide students to understand the information presented in the graph on page 184.

Investigate, p. 179

Before students begin the Investigate:

- Remind students of what they have learned about food chains. Invite a volunteer to suggest a food chain from the choices given. Record it by saying each component as you write.
- Have volunteers use this information to draw in the arrows. Follow the same procedures for a second food chain,
- Help students to understand what the term *overlap* means in step 5.
- Ask students to discuss how it is easier to understand a food web by studying a *model* of it than it is to directly observe animals interacting in the wild.

Modify Instruction—Multilevel Strategies

Language and Vocabulary Students may not be familiar with the use of the term *blend* as it is used in this lesson. Explain that this word has several meanings. Some students may know its meaning *to mix*, as when blending the ingredients of a recipe. In this lesson, the word refers to the way a living thing hides itself because it looks much like its surrounding. An animal may blend in by color, such as that of an Arctic fox. An animal may also blend in by pattern, such as that of the stripes of a tiger. The following exercises provide opportunities to develop the lesson's use of this term.

Beginning Display three pictures of animals in different settings. Have one photograph show an animal blending with its surrounding, such as a chameleon on a leaf or an Arctic hare in snow. The other images should show animals that do not exhibit protective coloration. Invite students to point to the animal that *blends* with its surroundings.

© Harcourt

Intermediate Point to each picture in turn and ask students, "Does the animal blend with its surroundings?" Have students repeat either "The animal blends with its surroundings" or "The animal does not blend with its surroundings."

Advanced Invite students to identify whether each picture shows an animal blending in with its surroundings or not. Have them justify their answers by telling why, or why not.

For All Students Help students to see that animals have other ways of defending themselves in order to survive.

Extend

Have students complete the **Show What You Know** activity on page 71 to demonstrate their understanding of food webs.

③ Apply and Assess

Make a Drawing

When to Use	Proficiency Levels
With Reading Review p. 185	✔ Beginning
	✔ Intermediate
🕐 20 minutes	✔ Advanced

Materials: drawing paper, old nature magazines, crayons and colored pencils, scissors, tape

- Have students use old nature magazines to find and cut out a picture of an animal that is known to blend in with its surroundings. Some examples include tigers, lions, deer, rattlesnakes, flounder, leafhoppers, ptarmigans, bitterns, and toads.
- Have them tape the picture onto the drawing paper and, using colored pencils or crayons, draw a scene around the animal in which the animal blends in with its surroundings.
- Display and discuss the pictures.

Informal Assessment

Beginning	Intermediate	Advanced
Show students two pictures of animals—one that blends in with its surroundings and one that does not. Ask them to point to the picture that shows an animal *blending* into its surroundings. *(Answer: Students should identify the correct picture.)*	Have students copy and complete the following sentence frame. One way that an animal defends itself is to _____ in with its surroundings. *(Answer: blend)*	Have students copy and complete this sentence. An animal blends into its surroundings when it _____. *(Answers will vary. Possible answer: has the same color as its surroundings.)*

Name _____

Date _____

Draw a Food Web

Draw a food web with at least two different food chains. Then, draw an
arrow or arrows to show where the food chains overlap to form a food web.

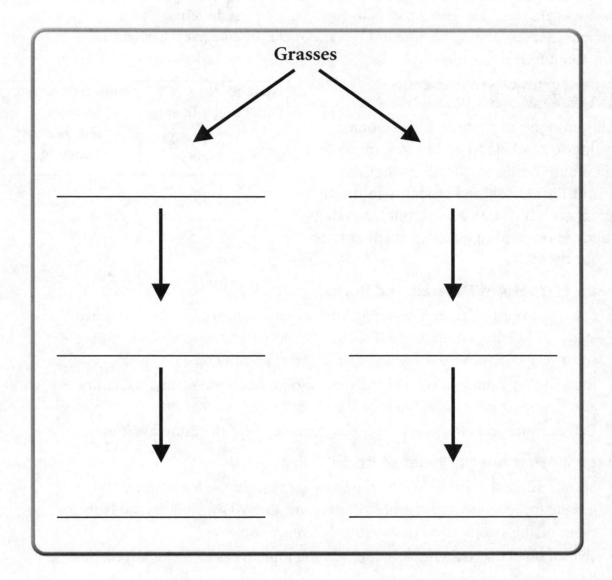

School-Home Connection: Have students take this page home to share with
family members. They can use their pictures to tell about food chains and food webs.

6 Minerals and Rocks

Develop Scientific Concepts and Vocabulary

In this chapter, students will learn the difference between minerals and rocks, how rocks are classified into three main types (igneous, sedimentary, and metamorphic), and how the different types of rocks are formed. They will also learn about fossil formation.

Preview Scientific Principles

Walk through the chapter with students, pausing to read aloud or to have volunteers read aloud the three questions that are lesson titles. Encourage students to briefly discuss each question and to tell what they already know that might help them answer the questions.

When to Use With Chapter Opener	Proficiency Levels
🕐 20 minutes	✔ Beginning ✔ Intermediate ✔ Advanced

Lesson 1: What Are Minerals and Rocks?

- Show examples of several minerals, such as salt, iron, gold, graphite (pencil lead), and perhaps a diamond. Explain that although these substances may seem very different from one another, they are all minerals.
- Explain that a mineral is an object that is solid, has been formed by nature, and has never been alive. Rocks are made of minerals.
- Call on volunteers to explain how people use each of the mineral samples.

Lesson 2: What Are the Types of Rocks?

- Show samples of the three rock types, such as sandstone for sedimentary, granite for igneous, and marble for metamorphic. Allow time for students to examine the samples and discuss the differences they see.
- Tell students that the samples represent the three types of rocks and that the differences they observe are a result of how the rocks were formed.
- Ask students to name some ways that people use rocks.
- Ask if any students have rock collections that they might share with the class.

© Harcourt

Lesson 3: What Are Fossils?

- Show several fossils. Allow time for students to examine them and discuss what they see.
- Explain that these are fossils, made by plants or animals long ago. Fossils are found in rocks. Ask if students have ever seen fossils in museums or in nature.
- Explain that scientists study fossils to find out what kinds of plants and animals lived long ago. By learning about prehistoric plants and animals, scientists can know more about what Earth was like long ago and how it has changed.

Practice

Create the chart below on the board. For the second column, have students tell you what they think each word means. Then they will dictate ways they can learn more about each word, such as studying the chapter, looking at the illustrations, and so on.

Word	What I think it means	How I can learn more
mineral rock fossil		

Apply

Read the following riddles aloud, and have students work together to answer them.

Rock Riddles

I am a footprint left by a dinosaur. What am I? (fossil)
I am granite and marble. What am I? (rock)
I am salt and pencil lead. What am I? (mineral)
I am the outline of a leaf on a rock. What am I? (fossil)
I am made of minerals. What am I? (rock)
I am gold and diamonds. What am I? (mineral)

Lesson 1 — What Are Minerals and Rocks?

① Build Background

Access Prior Knowledge

When to Use	Proficiency Levels
Before introducing the lesson 15 minutes	✔ Beginning ✔ Intermediate Advanced

Write *mineral* and *rock* on the board. Give students an opportunity to tell what they know about minerals and rocks. List phrases or draw sketches on the board to summarize their responses. Ask where minerals and rocks are often found.

Preteach Lesson Vocabulary

mineral, rock

Materials: salt, piece of pencil lead

List the vocabulary words on the board.

Have students look at page 198 and see if they can find either of these words. Repeat on page 202 for the word *rock*. Explain that the highlighted, boldfaced words in the text mean that a definition was just given or will follow. Then:

- Place a small pile of salt and a piece of pencil lead on a desk.
- Call for volunteers to identify one or both as minerals. *Both are minerals.*
- Introduce the word *mineral* by defining it as something that is solid, formed in nature, and has never been alive.
- Ask students what they think the word *rock* means. Lead them to conclude that rock is made of one or more minerals. It, too, is solid, formed in nature, and has never been alive.

Build Fluency

Have students work in pairs to complete pairs of sentence frames such as the following:

1. A _____ is an object that has never been _____. (*mineral or rock, alive*)
2. A _____ is made of one or more _____. (*rock, minerals*)

© Harcourt

② Scaffold the Content

Preview the Lesson

When to Use With pp. 197–202	Proficiency Levels
⏱ 20 minutes	✔ Beginning ✔ Intermediate ✔ Advanced

- Ask students to point to the title on page 196 as you read it aloud. Explain that they will find the answer to this question in the lesson. Have students scan the section headings to preview the location of the answer.
- Have students look at the pictures on pages 198 through 202 and describe the similarities or differences they see.
- Point out that hardness and color are two ways to tell one mineral from another.
- Write *Mohs Scale* on the board and have students find this term on page 200.
- Explain that the scale is named after Frederich Mohs, the scientist who created it.
- Ask students how the scale could help identify minerals.

Investigate, p. 197

Before students begin the Investigate:

- Point out that the *Procedure* is a list of steps that tells them what to do. If they have trouble reading the directions, encourage them to refer to the table and the photograph.
- If necessary, demonstrate how to scratch one mineral with another. Explain that *record* means to write down what they see. Consider writing some of the students' observations on the board to model how to record them.
- Urge students to wear safety goggles as they work.
- Have partners complete the activity. Afterward, discuss what students did and have volunteers answer aloud the questions on page 197.

Modify Instruction—Multilevel Strategies

Background/Experience The identification of rocks and minerals involves understanding that they have different properties that can be observed and classified. The following activities provide opportunities for students to recognize how they use classification in their daily lives.

Beginning On small, separate pieces of paper, have the students draw geometric shapes—triangles, rectangles, circles, ovals, and so on. Then, ask them to observe each piece of paper and classify, or sort, the papers according to how many corners the shapes have.

© Harcourt

Intermediate Write headings, such as *food*, *clothes*, and *people* on the board. Then, name an item to be classified, such as *apple*, *socks*, or *father*. Have students tell you under which heading to write that item. Continue with other items. Then, encourage students to name items that can be classified under one of these headings.

Advanced Ask students to turn to page 200. Point out that rocks are classified by their color and hardness. Write *soft*, *hard*, and *very hard* as headings on the board. Have students suggest items that could be listed under each heading. For example, *cotton* is soft, *books* are hard, and *concrete* is very hard.

For All Students Have students work together to make a word map with the words *mineral*, *rock*, and *fossil*. Encourage them to suggest words and phrases that you can connect to each word. They might add to this word map as they progress through the lesson.

Extend

Have the students complete the Show What You Know activity on page 77 to demonstrate their understanding of rocks and minerals. *(Answers: I. halite 2. gold, copper 3. gold, diamond, garnet 4. granite 5. graphite 6. quartz)*

③ Apply and Assess

Make a Rock Collection

Materials: drawing supplies or old magazines, scissors, poster board, tape

When to Use With Reading Review p. 203 20 minutes	Proficiency Levels ✔ Beginning ✔ Intermediate ✔ Advanced

- Have groups of three work together to draw or cut out magazine pictures of different kinds of minerals, from salt to graphite to diamonds.
- Ask students to group pictures of similar types of minerals on poster board and label the page.

Informal Assessment

Beginning	Intermediate	Advanced
Have each student name a kind of mineral. *(Answers may include mica, garnet, tanzanite, quartz, gold, graphite, or other minerals.)*	Have each student name a way to classify minerals. *(Answers may include hardness, streak, color, or other properties.)*	Have each student write two sentences about how minerals are classified. *(Answers will vary.)*

© Harcourt

Name _____

Date _____

Following the Clues

Read each clue and decide which rock or mineral it describes. Write the
name of the rock or mineral. One answer can be used twice.

garnet	**quartz**	**graphite**	**halite**
granite	**gold**	**copper**	**diamond**

1. A mineral that we eat _____

2. Two minerals used as money _____

_____

3. Three minerals used as jewelry _____

_____ _____

4. A rock made of several minerals _____

5. A mineral that helps us write _____

6. A mineral used to make glass _____

School-Home Connection: Have students take this page home to share with
family members. They can use this page to share what they have learned about
rocks and minerals.

Lesson 2 — What Are the Types of Rocks?

① Build Background

Access Prior Knowledge

When to Use	Proficiency Levels
Before introducing the lesson	✔ Beginning
🕐 15 minutes	✔ Intermediate
	Advanced

Encourage students to share what they know about types of rocks. Ask them to describe rocks they have seen and ways those rocks were similar or different. Ask how they think rocks form.

Preteach Lesson Vocabulary

igneous rock, sedimentary rock, metamorphic rock

Materials: samples of the three types of rocks

List the vocabulary words on the board.

Have students look at pages 206 and 207 and find the terms on the board. Ask a volunteer to read the definition that follows each term. Then:

- Display a sample of all three types of rock.
- Invite volunteers to point out ways in which the samples are similar and different.
- Remind students that rocks are made of minerals.
- Point out that the word *igneous* has to do with heat or fire, the word *sediment* means small pieces, and the word *metamorphic* refers to change.

Build Fluency

Have pairs complete sentence frames such as the following:

1. The word *ignite* is like the word _____. *(igneous)*
2. Small pieces of soil are called _____. *(sediment)*

Use similar sentences to clarify the meaning of *igneous*, *sedimentary*, and *metamorphic*.

② Scaffold the Content

When to Use	Proficiency Levels
With pp. 206–212	✔ Beginning
🕐 15 minutes	✔ Intermediate
	✔ Advanced

Preview the Lesson

- Ask students to point to the title on page 204 as you read it aloud. Explain that they will find the answer to this question in the lesson. Ask how they think the cliffs were formed. Encourage them to describe other cliffs they have seen.

- Ask students to look at the pictures on pages 206 through 212. Ask which pictures show different types of rocks and which show ways in which rocks are formed. Guide students to recognize that page 211 shows how rocks change from one type to another.

Investigate, p. 205

Before students begin the Investigate:

- Review the steps in the Procedure and ask volunteers to explain what they will do in their own words. Direct students to the photographs for additional help.

- Make sure students understand the terms *spoonful* and *lump*.

- Have partners complete the activity. Afterward, discuss what students did and have volunteers answer aloud the questions on page 205.

Modify Instruction—Multilevel Strategies

Comprehensible Input The following activities provide opportunities for students to better understand the three types of rock formation. Write *igneous rock*, *sedimentary rock*, and *metamorphic rock* on the board.

Beginning Use rock samples, pictures, words, and gestures to pantomime the three kinds of rock formation: heat (igneous), pressure (sedimentary), and heat and pressure (metamorphic). Read each term and have students repeat it as you act out the process.

Intermediate Use rock samples, words, and gestures to pantomime the three kinds of rock formation. Then, invite volunteers to pantomime each kind and name it.

© Harcourt

Advanced Explain that during the Investigate students made sedimentary rock, although they did not squeeze it together. To help explain igneous rock formation, ask volunteers to identify things that melt when heated and then become solid as they cool, such as cheese. Explain that metamorphic rock forms by pressure and heat deep inside Earth.

For All Students Invite volunteers to pantomime the formation of one kind of rock. The class will then identify that type by naming it or pointing to the term on the board. Have volunteers describe the formation in their own words.

Extend

Have the students complete the **Show What You Know** activity on page 81 to demonstrate their knowledge of the rock cycle.

③ Apply and Assess

Make a Mural

When to Use	Proficiency Levels
With Reading Review p. 213	✔ Beginning
	✔ Intermediate
🕐 30 minutes	✔ Advanced

- Organize three groups and assign each group one type of rock formation. That group will create a mural showing examples of its type of rock and explaining how that type forms. Have the groups use labels and captions to explain the process.
- Display the murals on the classroom walls and have each group summarize its mural for the class. Discuss how the murals are similar and different.

Informal Assessment

Beginning	Intermediate	Advanced
Have each student name or point to a picture of an example of each type of rock. (*Answers may include granite or obsidian for igneous rock, sandstone or limestone for sedimentary rock, and marble or gneiss for metamorphic rock.*)	Have each student give an example of a force of nature that helps in rock formation. (*Answers may include the heat inside Earth or in volcanoes, the pressure of many layers of rock, and wind and water that break rock into bits.*)	Have each student write three sentences. Each sentence should describe how a certain type of rock is formed. (*Possible answers: Igneous rock is formed when rock melts and then cools. Sedimentary rock is formed when layers of bits of rock harden into new rock. Metamorphic rock is formed by pressure and heat deep inside Earth.*)

Name _____

Date _____

The Rock Cycle

Draw a diagram of the rock cycle. Then label your diagram with words from the list below.

igneous	**heat**	**water**
sedimentary	**pressure**	**melting**
metamorphic	**wind**	**cooling**

© Harcourt

School-Home Connection: Have students take this page home to share with family members. They may refer to the page as they search near their homes for examples of the three types of rocks.

Lesson 3 **What Are Fossils?**

① Build Background

Access Prior Knowledge

Encourage students to share what they know about fossils. Ask them to describe fossils they have seen in museums or in nature.

When to Use	Proficiency Levels
Before introducing the lesson ⏱ 15 minutes	✔ Beginning ✔ Intermediate Advanced

Preteach Lesson Vocabulary

Write the vocabulary word on the board.

fossil

- Have students find the word *fossil* on page 216.
- Invite a volunteer to read the definition aloud.
- Ask students what the photos on pages 216 and 217 tell them about fossils.

Build Fluency

Have pairs complete sentence frames such as the following:

1. A _____ is a trace of a living thing that died a long time ago. *(fossil)*

2. In some fossils, bones are replaced by _____. *(minerals)*

Ask students to use similar sentences to clarify the definition of *fossil*.

© Harcourt

② Scaffold the Content

Preview the Lesson

- Ask students to point to the title on page 214 as you read it aloud. Explain that they will find the answer to this question in the lesson. Have students name other prehistoric animals that might have left fossils behind. Ask how people find fossils.
- Have students scan the pictures on pages 216 through 220. Ask which pictures show types of fossils and which show how fossils are formed.
- Write *mold* on the board and have students find this word on page 217.
- Use clay and an object to show that a mold is the empty space left behind after the organism that made it dissolves.
- Then write *cast* on the board and have students find this word on page 217.
- Explain that the object that made the mold is the cast.

Investigate, p. 215

Before students begin the Investigate:

- Read the procedure aloud and have a volunteer show how to complete each step (or complete each step yourself).
- Make sure students understand the words *coat, model, drizzle,* and *imprint.*
- Invite volunteers to describe other models they have made, such as model airplanes.
- Have students explain what they will do in the Investigate in their own words.
- Have partners complete the activity. Afterward, discuss what students did and have volunteers answer aloud the questions on page 215.

Modify Instruction—Multilevel Strategies

Language/Vocabulary Introduce the concept of compound words. Explain that two words, such as *sea* and *shell,* can be combined to form the new word *seashell.*

Beginning On the board, draw and label the sea, an eggshell, and a seashell. Have students repeat the three words after you and underline shared letters.

© Harcourt

Intermediate Write several compound words on the board and read them aloud. (Examples: *goldfish, birdhouse, backpack, bedroom*) Help students find the short words in each compound. Explain their meanings and the meaning of the compound word. Have pairs choose a word to illustrate and define.

Advanced Ask students to suggest other compound words. Have them explain the meanings of the root words and the compound word. Ask them to use the compound words in sentences.

For All Students Write *side* and *walk* on the board. Ask students to read the words aloud or say them after you. Then discuss what each word means and what they mean when they are joined together.

Extend

Have the students complete the Show What You Know activity on page 85 to demonstrate their understanding of fossils.

③ Apply and Assess

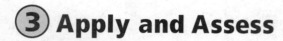

Materials: clay, classroom objects chosen by students

When to Use With Reading Review p. 221	Proficiency Levels
🕐 20 minutes	✔ Beginning ✔ Intermediate ✔ Advanced

- Have pairs of students use a classroom object and clay to make a "fossil"— without letting other students see which object they used.

- Ask pairs to exchange "fossils" and try to identify the object that made the imprint.

Informal Assessment

Beginning	Intermediate	Advanced
Have each student name a fossil mentioned in the text. *(Answers will vary.)*	Have each student explain how studying fossils helps scientists. *(Answers will vary.)*	Have each student write two sentences that summarize the best conditions for fossil formation. *(Answers will vary.)*

© Harcourt

Name _____

Date _____

Finding Fossils

Write about a place near your home that might be good for fossil hunting. Explain why you chose that place. Then draw a picture of it.

_____

_____

_____

_____

School-Home Connection: Have students take this page home to share with family members. They can use it to encourage family members to join them on a fossil hunt.

7 Forces That Shape the Land

Develop Scientific Concepts and Vocabulary

In this chapter, students will learn about landforms and the processes that change them either slowly or quickly.

Preview Scientific Principles

Walk through the chapter with students, pausing to read aloud or to have volunteers read aloud the three questions that are lesson titles. Encourage students to briefly discuss each question and to tell what they already know that might help them answer the questions.

When to Use With Chapter Opener	Proficiency Levels
20 minutes	✔ Beginning ✔ Intermediate ✔ Advanced

Lesson 1: What Are Landforms?

- Preview the pictures in the lesson with students. Point out that there are many types of landforms.
- Explain that landforms are created and changed in different ways and by different natural forces.
- Call on volunteers to give examples of different landforms near the area where you live.

Lesson 2: How Do Landforms Change Slowly?

- Ask students what happens to sand when waves wash up on a beach.
- Ask students what happens to small particles of dust or sand on a windy day.
- Explain to students that, over time, water and wind can change landforms by acting on even large, hard pieces of rock.
- Briefly explain to students what glaciers are and how they scrape the surface of Earth.

Lesson 3: How Do Landforms Change Quickly?

- Ask for volunteers to explain what an earthquake is. Discuss and clarify their ideas about earthquakes.

© Harcourt

- Ask for volunteers to explain what a volcano is. Discuss and clarify their ideas about volcanoes.
- Ask for volunteers to explain what a flood is. Discuss and clarify their ideas about floods.
- Explain that earthquakes, volcanoes, and floods are three Earth forces that can cause dramatic changes in landforms in very short amounts of time.

Practice

To help students use vocabulary from the chapter's topic, involve them in contributing to a giant word web around the word *LANDFORM* on the board. Encourage students to dictate or write related words around the focus word.

Have students choose words from the web to use in sentences about landforms. Encourage them to use words from the board in their sentences. Then ask for volunteers to read their sentences aloud.

Apply

List the title *Landforms* on a large sheet of easel paper. Below it, write *How They Change Slowly* and *How They Change Quickly*. With students, brainstorm the ways that land changes and whether they are quick or slow changes. Then list the vocabulary words from the chart below. Read the words to students. Have students copy the words into a notebook or on lined paper. Tell students to write the definitions as they learn more.

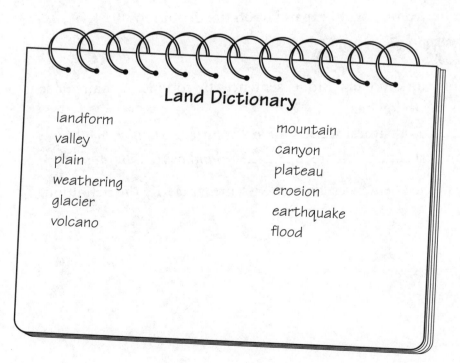

Land Dictionary

landform
valley
plain
weathering
glacier
volcano

mountain
canyon
plateau
erosion
earthquake
flood

What Are Landforms?

① Build Background

Access Prior Knowledge

When to Use	Proficiency Levels
Before introducing the lesson	✔ Beginning
🕐 15 minutes	✔ Intermediate
	Advanced

- Give students an opportunity to use sentences as they talk about their ideas about landforms.
- Ask students to give examples of landforms they have seen near where they live.
- Ask students if they know the names of some landforms.

Preteach Lesson Vocabulary

> **landform, mountain, valley, canyon, plain, plateau**

List the vocabulary words on the board.

Have students look at page 232 and tell where any words on the board are on the page.

- Ask for a volunteer to stand with you in front of the group.
- Have the volunteer read the words on the board out loud.
- Invite students to offer definitions of the board words.
- Call on other volunteers to expand upon the definitions.

Build Fluency

Have students work in pairs. Model sentences by completing pairs of sentence frames such as the following:

1. A _____ is a natural shape on Earth's surface. *(landform)*
2. Earth's highest _____ are _____. *(landforms; mountains)*

Ask students to use sentences like these to further clarify the definition of landforms.

© Harcourt

② Scaffold the Content

Preview the Lesson

When to Use With pp. 230–236	Proficiency Levels
⏱ 15 minutes	✔ Beginning ✔ Intermediate Advanced

Ask students to point to the title on page 230 as you read it aloud. Explain that they will find the answer to this question in the lesson. Have students discuss the picture on page 230. Have students give their ideas about how rock might be pressed and folded.

Have students preview the pictures on pages 232–236 and summarize what they see.

- Explain that most of the pictures show types of landforms, while the picture on page 232 shows Earth's internal layers.
- Write *crust* on the board and have students find it on page 232. Discuss the word.
- Explain how Earth's surface layer is similar to the crust on a loaf of bread.

Investigate, p. 231

Before the students begin the Investigate, demonstrate the Procedure. Then have students work in teams to complete the activity.

- Ask students to tell what they did to complete the activity. Help them draw conclusions by asking volunteers to answer aloud the activity questions.
- To further develop the lesson concepts, you may want to build comprehension and provide meaning for some of the other important technical words. Say aloud the words you choose, using each in a context sentence, and provide its meaning. Then have students repeat the word and find it in their texts.

Modify Instruction—Multilevel Strategies

Language and Vocabulary To explore and clarify how words in the English language work, introduce the concept of borrowed words, using the word *mesa* (table) as an example. Explain that many words from many different languages have become part of the English language vocabulary.

Beginning Have students draw a picture of a table and compare it to a plateau, which is defined as a flat area higher than the land around it. Ask them how the word *mesa* might come to be used to describe a small plateau. Point out that borrowed words usually enter the English language through frequent use.

© Harcourt

Intermediate Write several borrowed words on the board. Read the words aloud and give their meanings as students repeat after you. Have student pairs choose a word to write down and illustrate. Then have students define the words in their own terms.

Advanced Ask students to think of other borrowed words. Encourage them to refer to their own family heritage or other background knowledge in becoming aware of borrowed words. Have them pick a word and write it in a sentence.

For All Students Ask students to turn to page 230. Call on volunteers to tell how a mesa is like a table. Then call on volunteers to compare other landforms to household objects.

Extend

Have the students complete the **Show What You Know** activity on page 91 to demonstrate their understanding of landforms.

③ Apply and Assess

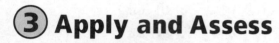

Make a Landform

Materials: any available molding or building materials

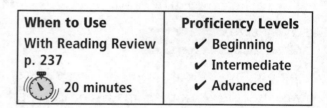

When to Use	Proficiency Levels
With Reading Review p. 237 20 minutes	✔ Beginning ✔ Intermediate ✔ Advanced

- Have students in groups of three to five pick a landform, then work together to create simple models.
- Have other students guess what each model is intended to represent.
- Ask the groups to join in putting their models together to form their own imaginary continent. Encourage them to use geographic maps as reference.

Informal Assessment

Beginning	Intermediate	Advanced
Have each student give an example of a landform mentioned in the text. *(Answers will vary.)*	Have each student give an example of a way in which landforms can be changed. *(Answers will vary.)*	Have each student write two sentences that summarize the ways in which landforms can be changed slowly and quickly. *(Answers will vary.)*

© Harcourt

Name _____

Date _____

Telling About Landforms

Finish each sentence below.

A landform is _____

_____

A mountain is _____

_____

A valley is _____

_____

A canyon is _____

_____

A plain is _____

_____

A plateau is _____

_____

School-Home Connection: Have students take this page home to share with family members. They can use their sentences to tell about landforms.

© Harcourt

2 How Do Landforms Change Slowly?

1 Build Background

Access Prior Knowledge

When to Use	Proficiency Levels
Before introducing the lesson	✔ Beginning
🕐 15 minutes	✔ Intermediate
	Advanced

- Give students an opportunity to use sentences as they talk about their ideas about how landforms change over time.
- Ask them to give examples of landforms they have seen.
- Ask them what natural forces might cause landforms to change slowly.

Preteach Lesson Vocabulary

weathering, erosion, glacier

Materials: sand, sandstone

List the vocabulary words on the board.

Have students look at page 240 and tell where any words on the board are on the page. Then:

- Place a small pile of sand and a piece of sandstone on a desk.
- Call for volunteers to identify the materials.
- Introduce the concept of *weathering* by explaining that the sandstone can be broken down into individual grains of sand over time.
- Ask students for their ideas about how individual grains of sand could join to form sandstone.

Build Fluency

Have students work in pairs. Model sentences by completing pairs of sentence frames, such as the following:

1. _____ is the way rocks are broken down into smaller pieces. *(Weathering)*
2. _____ and _____ are two things that cause weathering. *(Wind; water)*

Ask students to use sentences like these to further clarify the weathering process.

© Harcourt

③ Scaffold the Content

Preview the Lesson

When to Use	Proficiency Levels
With pp. 238–244	✔ Beginning
⏱ 15 minutes	✔ Intermediate
	Advanced

Call attention to the title on page 238 as you read it aloud. Explain that the lesson will answer this question. Have students examine the picture. Call for volunteers to answer the question in the Fast Fact box. Then discuss the answers.

Preview the pictures on pages 240–244. Have students note similarities and differences.

- Explain that the pictures show examples of ways landforms can change slowly.
- Point out that water is often involved in slow landform changes.
- Have students find *erosion* on page 242. Discuss erosion. Explain that the soil carried by rivers is called *sediment*.

Investigate, p. 239

Before the students begin the Investigate, allow time for students to examine the pieces of brick at close hand. Then have students work with partners to complete the activity.

- Ask students to tell what they did to complete the activity. Help them draw conclusions by asking volunteers to answer aloud the activity questions.
- To further develop the lesson concepts and build comprehension, provide meanings for some of the other technical words, such as *mass*, *delta*, *creep*, and *sand dune*. Read the chosen words aloud, using each in a context sentence, and provide its meaning. Then have students repeat the word and find it in their texts.

Modify Instruction—Multilevel Strategies

Background/Experience The slow changing of landforms, the focus of this lesson, involves understanding the concepts of weathering and erosion. Learners will benefit by associating these concepts with their own daily activities. The following activities provide opportunities for students to recognize examples of weathering and erosion in their own daily lives.

Beginning Have students draw a series of pictures of the stages of erosion of a mountain. The first picture should show a tall, craggy mountain, the second a slightly smaller and less craggy one, until the last picture is a small hill or flat land.

Intermediate Have students copy from the board simple sentences about weathering and erosion. Read each sentence aloud, having students read along or echo the sentences. Invite partners to choose one sentence to copy and illustrate. Then have students act out their sentences for the group to guess.

Advanced Ask students to turn to page 244 and examine the bar graph. Call on volunteers to read the questions. Then call on volunteers to answer the questions. Encourage discussion of the answers to the questions.

For All Students Direct the students to the picture of a delta on page 242. Ask students to give their ideas about why the delta takes the shape of a fan. Encourage discussion.

Extend

Have the students complete the **Show What You Know** activity on page 95 to demonstrate their understanding of the way landforms change slowly.

③ Apply and Assess

Write a Report

When to Use	Proficiency Levels
With Reading Review p. 245 ⏱ 20 minutes	✔ Beginning ✔ Intermediate Advanced

- Have students in groups of three to five work together to find out more about sand dunes.

- Have them organize their research and write it in the form of a report.

- Ask the groups to share their reports by reading them aloud. Then write a comprehensive summary of all the facts the students learned on the board.

Informal Assessment

Beginning	Intermediate	Advanced
Have each student give an example of a type of weathering process. *(Answers will vary.)*	Have each student give an example of how weathering might change a landform. *(Answers will vary.)*	Have each student write two sentences about the process of erosion. *(Answers will vary.)*

© Harcourt

Matching Landform Changes

Match the word on the top with the definition on the bottom. Write the
number of the word on the line next to the definition.

1. weathering
2. erosion
3. glacier
4. delta
5. creep
6. sand dune

_____ a huge block of ice

_____ soil dropped at the mouth of a river

_____ movement of weathered rock and soil

_____ a big pile of sand

_____ the way rocks are broken down into smaller pieces

_____ a very slow type of erosion

School-Home Connection: Have students take this page home to share
with family members. They can use their definitions to tell about how landforms
change slowly.

3 How Do Landforms Change Quickly?

1 Build Background

Access Prior Knowledge

When to Use	Proficiency Levels
Before introducing the lesson	✔ Beginning
🕐 15 minutes	✔ Intermediate
	Advanced

- Give students an opportunity to use sentences as they talk about their ideas about ways in which landforms change quickly.
- Ask them to give examples of rapid landform changes they have seen, and ways in which the landforms changed.
- Ask them what natural forces caused the rapid change.

Preteach Lesson Vocabulary

> earthquake, volcano, flood

Materials: rocks

List the vocabulary words on the board.

Have students look at page 248 and tell where any words on the board are on the page. Then:

- Arrange several pieces of rock in a large plastic bowl.
- Invite students to examine the arrangement of the rocks.
- Shake the bowl with a sudden, swift motion.
- Invite students to examine the rocks again, noting how their arrangement has changed.

Build Fluency

Have students work in pairs. Model sentences by completing pairs of sentence frames, such as the following:

1. An _____ is the shaking of Earth's surface. *(earthquake)*
2. Earthquakes are caused by movement in Earth's _____. *(crust)*

Ask students to use sentences like these for the words *earthquake*, *volcano*, and *flood*.

© Harcourt

② Scaffold the Content

Preview the Lesson

When to Use With pp. 246–252	Proficiency Levels
⏱ 15 minutes	✔ Beginning ✔ Intermediate Advanced

Call attention to the title on page 246 as you read it aloud. Explain that the lesson will answer this question. Encourage students to discuss the picture.

Preview the pictures on pages 248 through 252, and ask students to tell about them.

- Explain that many of the pictures show how quick landform change can cause destruction or damage to structures and to people.
- Ask students to predict which cause of quick landform change is most destructive, based on looking at the pictures. Encourage group discussion.
- Ask students what melted rock at Earth's surface is called.

Investigate, p. 247

Before the students begin the Investigate, allow students to become familiar with the materials. Then have students complete the activity.

- Ask students to tell what they did to complete the activity. Help them draw conclusions by asking volunteers to answer aloud the activity questions.
- To further develop the lesson concepts and to build comprehension, provide meanings for some of the other technical words, such as *eruption*, *fault*, *landslide*, and *lava*. Read aloud the words you choose, using each in a context sentence, and provide its meaning. Then have students repeat the word and find it in their texts.

Modify Instruction—Multilevel Strategies

Comprehensible Input The concept of how landforms change quickly, the focus of this lesson, involves understanding that the three causes of quick landform change have different effects on both landforms and the people that inhabit them. Learners will benefit by associating this concept with their own daily activities. The following activities provide opportunities for students to recognize examples of the three causes of quick landform change in their own daily lives.

Beginning Ask for volunteers to give examples of times, perhaps after a heavy rain, when they have seen strong flows of water cause soft soil to collapse, or form pools on low-lying areas. Explain that these examples are like floods, only smaller.

Intermediate Have students copy from the board simple sentences about causes of quick landform change. Read each sentence aloud, having students read along or echo the sentences. Have students act out their sentences for the group to guess.

Advanced On the board, draw a central circle surrounded by three other circles and connected to them by lines. In the central circle, write "How Landforms Change Quickly." Have students copy this graphic organizer onto their own sheets of paper. They should complete it by writing the name of a cause of quick landform change in each outer circle.

For All Students Direct students to the drought picture on page 252. Ask for a volunteer to read the caption. Call on volunteers to describe when an area gets too much rain.

Extend

Have the students complete the Show What You Know activity on page 99 to demonstrate their understanding of the three causes of quick landform changes.

③ Apply and Assess

Make a Model Flood

Materials: soil, rocks, safety goggles, measuring spoons, water, lab aprons, measuring cups, large trays, wax paper

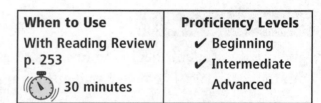

When to Use	Proficiency Levels
With Reading Review p. 253	✔ Beginning
⏱ 30 minutes	✔ Intermediate
	Advanced

- Have students in groups of three to five work together to create a model flood, similar to the modeling activities for earthquakes and volcanoes previously performed in the lesson.
- Stress that the models should be safe, and controlled so as not to make a mess.
- Assist students in gathering the materials they need for their models.
- Have student groups demonstrate finished models. Discuss ways in which they are similar or different.

Informal Assessment

Beginning	Intermediate	Advanced
Have each student give one example of a type of quick landform change. *(Answers will vary.)*	Have each student give an example of a quick landform change and its cause. *(Answers will vary.)*	Have each student write three sentences. Each sentence should summarize one of the three causes of quick landform changes. *(Answers will vary.)*

© Harcourt

Outlining Quick Landform Changes

Finish the outline below by filling in important facts about each cause of quick landform change.

I. Earthquakes

_____

_____

_____

II. Volcanoes

_____

_____

_____

III. Floods

_____

_____

_____

School-Home Connection: Have students take this page home to share with family members. They can use their outlines to tell about how landforms change quickly.

8 Conserving Resources

Develop Scientific Concepts and Vocabulary

In this chapter, students will learn about renewable and nonrenewable resources, layers and types of soil, how people's use of the environment changes it, and ways they can protect the environment.

Preview Scientific Principles

Walk through the chapter with students, pausing to read aloud or to have volunteers read aloud the four questions that are lesson titles. Encourage students to briefly discuss each question and to tell what they already know that might help them answer the questions.

When to Use With Chapter Opener	Proficiency Levels
🕐 20 minutes	✔ Beginning ✔ Intermediate ✔ Advanced

Lesson 1: What Are Some Types of Resources?

- Ask students to take a few deep breaths in and out. Ask them what resource they just used? Have students brainstorm about other resources they use in nature.

- Show students a renewable resource in the classroom, such as chalk or paper. Ask students what happens when all the chalk or paper is used up. Discuss this concept.

Lesson 2: What Are Some Types of Soil?

- Display a potted plant. Point to the soil and ask a volunteer to name it. Ask students what they know about soil and start a class list.

- Show some pictures of various types of soil. Point out the differences between them by asking yes/no questions. Add students' ideas to the class list.

Lesson 3: How Do People Use and Impact the Environment?

- Display pictures of pristine natural environments and have students examine them.

- Display photos of construction sites, logging camps, and mines. Ask students yes/no questions about what is happening in each photo and have them point to details.

- Invite students to talk about other ways people use the environment.

© Harcourt

Lesson 4: How Can Resources Be Used Wisely?

- Review with students the resources they've studied.
- Review the concept of pollution. Ask students to draw or explain what they think can be done to stop pollution and save resources.

Practice

To help students understand the concept of resources, talk about natural resources with students and about ways we use them in our daily lives. Have students create a natural resources collage or poster. Have them draw or cut pictures from magazines that show natural resources. Tape a large sheet of craft paper across the floor or wall. Have students paste their pictures on the paper. In the leftover spaces on the paper, have students draw ways they can save these resources.

Apply

Write the following words on slips of paper or index cards. Make enough to give each student or pair of students a word. Create a class T-chart with the headings *Resources* and *Recycle*. Ask students to read their words and think about which column on the chart they belong in. Invite volunteers to add their words to the chart. As each word is added, have students use it in simple sentences, such as, *Water is a resource. We recycle plastic.*

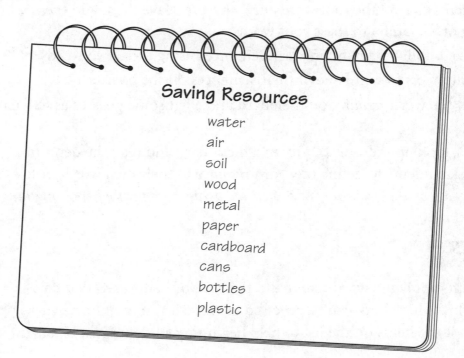

Saving Resources

water
air
soil
wood
metal
paper
cardboard
cans
bottles
plastic

Lesson 1 — What Are Some Types of Resources?

① Build Background

Access Prior Knowledge

When to Use	Proficiency Levels
Before introducing the lesson 15 minutes	✔ Beginning ✔ Intermediate ✔ Advanced

Allow students to talk about items they have used today. Start the discussion by making a statement, such as, "I used water to wash my face this morning." Have students help you list the items they used and then talk about how the items are alike or different.

Preteach Lesson Vocabulary

resource , renewable, reusable

List the vocabulary words on the board.

Have students find where the words on the board appear on pages 264–268.

- Draw divider lines through each word to separate the prefixes and suffixes in *renewable* and *reusable*.
- Remind students that the prefix *re-* means "again" or "to repeat."
- Ask students to read the root words *new* and *use*. Have them add the meaning of the prefix to these root words.
- Have mixed-ability pairs brainstorm sentences using these two words.
- Invite volunteers to write one of their sentences on the board.
- Point out the word *resource* on the board and elicit some guesses as to what it means.
- As a class, look up the word *source* in a dictionary and read the definition aloud. Ask students to define the word *resource* in their own words. Allow answers such as *the beginning of something again, to repeat where something comes from.*

Build Fluency

Help students apply the word *resource* to their list of items used that day, identifying which they think can be renewed or reused. You might prepare picture cards of the items on the list to help beginning students participate in this activity.

© Harcourt

② Scaffold the Content

Preview the Lesson

When to Use With pp. 262–268 20 minutes	Proficiency Levels ✔ Beginning ✔ Intermediate ✔ Advanced

- Ask students to follow along as you read the title on page 262 aloud. Tell them they will learn the answer to this question in this lesson.
- Have students look at the pictures on pages 264–268. Ask them to identify any resources they see in the photos by pointing to or naming what they see.
- Read each caption aloud as students follow along, verifying the resources in each photo.
- Lead a brief discussion of why animals, crops, trees, air, and coal are resources. Elicit how we use each of these resources.

Investigate, p. 263

Before students begin the Investigate, read the Procedure steps aloud as students follow along.

- Stop and focus on the words in quotation marks. Remind students that the quotation marks may mean that the word is being used in a way that is different from the usual meaning.
- Ask if students know what a *mine* is. Use the photo on page 268 to help clarify both the noun and verb forms of this word. Then reread step 3 of the Procedure and explain that students will pretend to "mine" the raisins from the cookie.

Modify Instruction—Multilevel Strategies

Language and Vocabulary Understanding renewable and nonrenewable resources, the focus of this lesson, involves recognition of adjectives and their common formations. Understanding the use of prefixes and suffixes to form adjectives aids students in their comprehension of scientific concepts. The following exercises provide opportunities to reinforce students' use of descriptive adjectives.

Beginning Provide students with flashcards of common root words, suffixes, and prefixes. Have them combine the flashcard words to make adjectives. Validate their words by using them in simple sentences.

Intermediate Have student pairs list at least three adjectives and then circle their root words. Ask them to use at least two of their adjectives in short sentences. Invite volunteers to share their sentences with the class.

Advanced Ask students to find the phrases *renewable resources* and *non-renewable resources* on pages 266–268 and write definitions of each in their own words.

For All Students Continue the lesson by reminding students to think about what makes renewable resources different from nonrenewable resources. Point out that the adjectives *renewable* and *nonrenewable* are good clues.

Extend

Have the students complete the **Show What You Know** activity on page 105. Students will demonstrate their understanding of descriptive adjectives.

③ Apply and Assess

Make Resource Trees

When to Use With Reading Review p. 269 🕐 30 minutes	Proficiency Levels ✔ Beginning ✔ Intermediate ✔ Advanced

Materials: magazines, scissors, construction paper, crayons or markers, paste

- Have students work in small groups to find and cut out magazine pictures of renewable resources.
- Direct them to draw a tree trunk at the center of their paper and then paste the pictures on the branches of the tree.
- Help students label their collages *Renewable Resources.*
- Have students repeat the steps above to make a second tree labeled *Nonrenewable Resources.*

Informal Assessment

Beginning	Intermediate	Advanced
Have each student point to three different resources in the room and tell whether they are renewable or nonrenewable. *(Answers will vary.)*	Have each student complete these sentences: Water is a _____ resource. Apples are a _____ resource. *(Answers: nonrenewable, renewable)*	Have each student write two sentences. Each sentence should tell about *what makes* a resource renewable or nonrenewable. *(Answers will vary.)*

© Harcourt

Describing Resources

Make adjectives by adding the prefixes and suffix to the root word in
each row.

Root Word	re-	-able	non-
new			

resources

use			

School-Home Connection: Have students take this page home to share with
family members. They can use it to tell about renewable and nonrenewable resources.

Lesson 2

What Are Some Types of Soil?

(1) Build Background

Access Prior Knowledge

When to Use	Proficiency Levels
Before introducing the lesson 10 minutes	✔ Beginning ✔ Intermediate Advanced

Materials: sand, potting soil, loam, 3 boxes, damp towels

Set out two or three different types of soil in separate boxes: sand, potting soil, and loam dug from the ground. Have students take turns digging their hands into each type of soil and letting it sift through their fingers. Provide some damp paper towels to clean students' hands before they return to their seats. Pick up a handful of each type of soil as you ask yes/no questions about how each one felt.

Preteach Lesson Vocabulary

humus, sand, loam, clay , silt

Materials: picture of forest floor, sample of humus, sand, and loam from previous activity

List the vocabulary words on the board.

Show students a picture of a forest floor. Ask students what they see. Ask what they think is under the top layer of fallen leaves and twigs and other natural material.

- Tell students that this natural material turns into soil over a long period of time. If possible, show them a sample of humus in which parts of leaves and other natural materials are still recognizable. Point to the word *humus* on the board and have students repeat it after you.
- Relate this soil to the samples. Ask which one they think has humus in it. *(loam)*
- Tell students that some soils are made of tiny pieces of rocks. Have students point to which sample they think is made of tiny pieces of rock and identify it as sand.
- Have students find the words on the board on pages 272–276. Tell them they will learn about types of soil in this lesson.

Build Fluency

Wave your hand over all the soil type samples and say *soil.* Point to samples or wave your hand over all as students say *sand, loam, soil* in chorus.

© Harcourt

② Scaffold the Content

Preview the Lesson

- Have students look at the picture on page 270 and follow along as you read the lesson title aloud. Remind students that they already know about two types of soil. Ask the class to name them. *(sand and loam)*

- Have students point to each subtitle on pages 272–276 as you read them aloud. Have them point to the highlighted words on each page. Invite volunteers to point to those same words on the board. Have the class say the words after you.

- Focus students' attention on the diagram on page 273. Have them point to each layer of soil and lead a discussion of what students notice about each layer.

Investigate, p. 271

Before the students begin the Investigate, pantomime the five senses with students as a review. Then, tell students they will use their eyes and fingers to observe the soil grains. On the board, write some descriptive words they might use to describe the soil samples.

Modify Instruction—Multilevel Strategies

Language and Vocabulary To help students fully comprehend the focus of the lesson, students will benefit from more in-depth exploration of the vocabulary they encounter in the lesson. Encourage students to use their index cards throughout the lesson to help them remember their new words.

Beginning Have students point to the words in the lesson they don't know. Ask them to copy each new word onto index cards and find a partner who can explain the words to them.

Intermediate Have students work in pairs to write new words from the lesson on index cards and then write a definition of each one in their own words.

Advanced Ask students to write new words from the lesson on index cards, look them up in a dictionary, and write a sentence using the word on the index card.

For All Students Continue the lesson by reminding students to look for new words as they learn about the layers of soil and different types of soil. Ask them to help each other understand new words.

© Harcourt

Have the students complete the **Show What You Know** activity on page 109. Students will demonstrate their understanding of layers of soil.

③ Apply and Assess

Create a Human Diagram

When to Use	Proficiency Levels
With Reading Review p. 277 🕐 15 minutes	✔ Beginning ✔ Intermediate ✔ Advanced

Tell students they will work together to model layers of soil. Divide the class into thirds.

- Have one group lie down on their sides on the floor, with one student's head to another's feet, in 2–3 rows. Elicit that they are bedrock.
- Have the second group lie curled up next to the first group on the floor, in 3 rows. Elicit that they are sand, silt, or clay and made from small bits of rock. Remind them to leave room for water to run through them.
- Have the last group lie flat on their backs, loose and splayed out next to the curled up students. Elicit that they are the topsoil: humus, sand, silt, and clay.
- Tell students you are a plant and ask where you should be to grow strong and healthy. Have students make room for your feet/roots in the topsoil layer.

Informal Assessment

Beginning	Intermediate	Advanced
Have students match their index cards with the vocabulary words on the board as you ask simple "this one or that one" questions about each type of soil. *(Answers will vary.)*	Have students create a short quiz on the words on their index cards. Ask them to write a question about the new word on each of their index cards. Then, have them rotate the cards and write the answers to their questions upside down below them. *(Answers will vary.)*	Have students write a short paragraph about what type of soil is best for growing plants, and why. *(Answers will vary.)*

New Words About Soil

In the box below, draw layers of soil. Label the parts of your drawing, using the new words you have learned.

Layers of Soil

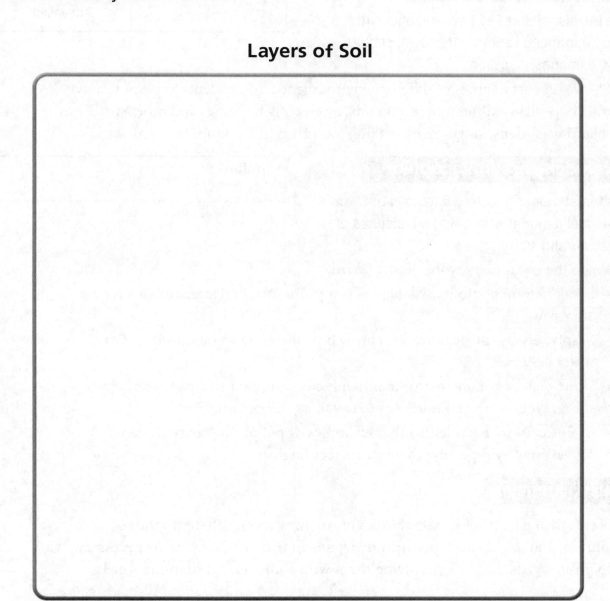

School-Home Connection: Have students take this page home to share with family members. They can use it to tell about types of soil.

How Do People Use and Impact the Environment?

Lesson 3

1 Build Background

Access Prior Knowledge

When to Use	Proficiency Levels
Before introducing the lesson 🕐 15 minutes	✔ Beginning ✔ Intermediate Advanced

Materials: pictures of environments with people in them: country, city, town, suburb, beach, mountain, desert

Show students pictures of different environments. Ask students to point to ways people have changed these environments, by erecting buildings and other structures, by planting gardens, and even by making footprints in the sand.

Preteach Lesson Vocabulary

> pollution

Materials: clear glass of water, bits of trash and small amount of cooking oil, pictures of clean air and smog

Write the vocabulary word on the board.

- Break *pollution* into its syllables as you pronounce it. Have students repeat after you.
- Display a glass of clean water. Throw bits of trash and oil into it and say *water pollution.*
- Show pictures of an environment with clean air next to a picture of city smog. Point to the polluted scene as you say *air pollution.*
- Brainstorm with students other examples of pollution. Verify students' suggestions by repeating them in correct English.

Build Fluency

Have small groups of mixed abilities create raps about different kinds of pollution, and ask them to perform their raps in front of the class. As necessary, help groups get started by supplying them with some related rhyming words.

② Scaffold the Content

When to Use	Proficiency Levels
With pp. 278–284	✔ Beginning
🕐 20 minutes	✔ Intermediate
	✔ Advanced

Preview the Lesson

- Ask students to follow along as you read the title on page 278 aloud. Tell students they will learn the answer in this lesson.
- Have students read the subheads and look at the photos on pages 280–284.
- Have students point to examples of different kinds of pollution in the pictures and name as many as they can.
- Use various forms of the word *pollute* in sentences as you talk about students' experiences with pollution.

Investigate, p. 279

Before the students begin the Investigate, have students point to the Investigate title and the words in the materials list as you read them aloud. Hold up each material and make sure students comprehend what they are to do.

Modify Instruction—Multilevel Strategies

Comprehensible Input Restating scientific concepts in different ways helps students with comprehension. Restate the main ideas on each page of the lesson. Provide other examples wherever possible. Use visuals to support the examples in the text. The following exercises will reinforce students' understanding of the focus of this lesson, people's use of the environment and of pollution.

Beginning Ask simple yes/no questions about each page in the lesson. Verify students' responses by restating them in complete sentences.

Intermediate Have pairs ask and answer questions about the content of each page. Invite them to interview other pairs in the class to create a list of examples of each type of pollution.

Advanced Have students write a brief summary of each page. Tell them to include specific examples, and remind them to use complete sentences. Invite volunteers to read their summaries aloud to the class.

For All Students Continue the lesson by reminding students that pollution is a bad result of people's use of the environment. Ask them to think about how pollution can be avoided.

Extend

Have the students complete the Show What You Know activity on page 113. Students will demonstrate their understanding of environmental uses and pollution.

③ Apply and Assess

Create Pollution Posters

When to Use	Proficiency Levels
With Reading Review p. 285	✔ Beginning
⏱ 10 minutes	✔ Intermediate
	✔ Advanced

Materials: drawing paper, crayons or markers, magazines for cutting, scissors, paste

Have small groups of mixed abilities create posters about people's use of the environment and resulting pollution.

- Distribute materials to each group. Direct students to choose one way that people use the environment. Remind them to think about how this changes the environment.
- Have them draw or paste pictures of this use and its results.
- Encourage them to include solutions to any pollution caused by this use.
- Remind students to title their posters.
- Display posters around the room and use them as discussion starters.

Informal Assessment

Beginning	Intermediate	Advanced
Have students draw and label three kinds of pollution. (*Answers: air, water, and land pollution*)	Have students complete the following sentence starters: When people throw trash on the ground, it _____ the land. Smoke from cars and factories causes air _____. Animals get sick in _____ water. (*Answers: pollutes, pollution, polluted*)	Have students write three complete sentences about causes of pollution. Ask them to suggest a way not to pollute the environment. (*Answers will vary.*)

© Harcourt

Name _____

Date _____

How People Change the Environment

1. In column 1, list four ways that people use the environment.

2. In column 2, write or draw a result of that use.

3. In column 3, rate the result by circling *good* or *bad*.

Use of Environment	Result	Rating
		good bad
		good bad
		good bad
		good bad

 School-Home Connection: Have students take this page home to share with family members. They can use it to tell about good and bad uses of the environment.

© Harcourt

How Can Resources Be Used Wisely?

① Build Background

Access Prior Knowledge

When to Use	Proficiency Levels
Before introducing the lesson 10 minutes	✔ Beginning ✔ Intermediate ✔ Advanced

Materials: drawing paper, crayons or markers

Ask students to list or draw things they use and then throw away. Have them add something they use over again instead of throwing it away. Brainstorm with students how some of the things they throw away could be used again or used for something else. Ask students why they think this might be a good idea.

Preteach Lesson Vocabulary

conservation, reduce, reuse, recycle

Materials: examples of trash and recyclable items

List the vocabulary words on the board.

- Show students the universal symbol for recycling, and ask volunteers to point to the word on the board they think it goes with. Point out the circular arrows on the symbol, and talk about how they symbolize the recycling process.
- Ask students to identify the kinds of things they put in recycle bins. As you hold up different items of trash, have students point to whether they would put the item in a trash can or a recycle bin.
- Ask how they might make less trash. Point to the word *reduce* on the board and explain that it means "to make less of." Ask how reducing trash can help save resources and protect the environment. Point to the word *conservation* and tell students it means "the saving of something," such as resources.
- Point to the word *reuse* on the board. Elicit its definition from students by breaking it down into its prefix and root word.

Build Fluency

Have students repeat the vocabulary words after you. Give each student an item for recycling, and ask them to chant the three verbs faster and faster as they walk in a circle around a recycle bin, tossing in their items one at a time. When the last item has been tossed, have them stop and stamp their feet in place as they proclaim "conservation!"

© Harcourt

② Scaffold the Content

Preview the Lesson

- Ask students to follow along as you read the title on page 286 aloud. Tell students they will learn the answer in this lesson.
- Have students look at the pictures on pages 288–292 and tell what they see.
- Have students point to the subheads on these pages as you read them aloud. Review what the vocabulary words mean.
- Ask students to find details in the pictures that illustrate these words.
- Have volunteers tell in their own words what this chapter is about.

Investigate, p. 287

Before students begin the Investigate, review words such as *weigh, weight, data,* and *graph* with students. Introduce the abbreviations for pound and feet, and make sure students understand the difference between *linear* and *weight measurements*. Use a yardstick and a scale to demonstrate, if necessary.

Modify Instruction—Multilevel Strategies

Background/Experience Relating students' personal experiences with conservation and recycling, the focus of this lesson, will help them make stronger connections with these concepts and aid their comprehension of the material.

Beginning Ask students to keep count of how many items they recycle in a day or a week. Have them add their numbers to a class list.

Intermediate Have students keep track of how many items they recycle and reuse in a week. Then have them answer yes/no questions about how they can reduce trash. Elicit that conservation of resources is important.

Advanced Ask students to keep track of how much they recycle and reuse in a week. Have them discuss ways they can reduce and reuse more items and why conservation of resources is important.

For All Students Continue the lesson by reminding students to think about all the ways they can help conserve resources.

Extend

Have the students complete the Show What You Know activity on page 117. Students will demonstrate their understanding of conservation techniques.

③ Apply and Assess

Make a Conservation Ad

Materials: heavy paper, crayons and markers

When to Use	Proficiency Levels
With Reading Review p. 293 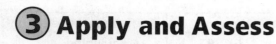 10 minutes	✔ Beginning ✔ Intermediate ✔ Advanced

Tell students they will create a full-page magazine advertisement to show people how to use resources wisely.

- Have students work in mixed ability pairs or groups. Distribute materials.
- Tell students to start by making a list of all the ways they've learned to reuse, reduce, and conserve resources.
- Ask them to choose three or four things from their list and plan how they will show them in their advertisement.
- Remind students to add words to their advertisement.

Informal Assessment

Beginning	Intermediate	Advanced
Have students draw two ways they used resources wisely this week. *(Answers will vary.)*	Have students act out two ways they used resources wisely this week. Ask them to identify if they are reusing, reducing, or recycling. *(Answers will vary.)*	Have students discuss how they use resources wisely and how they can help with conservation in the future. *(Answers will vary.)*

Name _____

Date _____

Measuring Conservation

Draw or write the items you recycle or reuse for three days. Then, count them up and write the total number in the last column.

	Recycle	Reuse	Totals
Day 1			
Day 2			
Day 3			

© Harcourt

School-Home Connection: Have students take this page home to share with family members. They can use it to tell about conservation of resources.

9 The Water Cycle

Develop Scientific Concepts and Vocabulary

In this chapter, students will learn about the importance of water and that it comes in three forms: solid, liquid, and gas. Students will also learn about the water cycle and the conditions that cause water to change forms. Finally, students will learn what weather is and how it is measured.

Preview Scientific Principles

Walk through the chapter with students, pausing to read aloud or to have volunteers read aloud the three questions that are lesson titles. Encourage students to briefly discuss each question and to tell what they already know that might help them answer the questions.

When to Use With Chapter Opener	Proficiency Levels
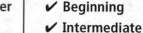 20 minutes	✔ Beginning ✔ Intermediate ✔ Advanced

Lesson 1: Where Is Water Found on Earth?

- Ask students to think of ways in which they use water and why it's important.
- Explain that water comes in different forms: *solid* (ice), *liquid* (water), and *gas* (water vapor). Prepare to discuss examples of each.
- Preview vocabulary by explaining that there is fresh water (in lakes, streams and underground), frozen water (in *glaciers*), and salt water (in the ocean).

Lesson 2: What Is the Water Cycle?

- The amount of water on Earth remains the same, but it changes form and moves from place to place. Draw a simple *water cycle* on the board. Explain that heat from sunlight causes water to become water vapor. It then cools and forms clouds. When water in clouds becomes too heavy, it falls to Earth as some form of *precipitation* and the process begins all over again.
- Changes in temperature cause water to change form. *Evaporation* of water occurs when the temperature increases sufficiently. *Condensation* occurs when the temperature falls sufficiently.

© Harcourt

Lesson 3: What Is Weather?

- Weather is the condition of the *atmosphere* at a certain place and time and is always changing.
- People use *thermometers* and other weather instruments to measure conditions in the atmosphere and to forecast changes in weather.

Practice

Have students brainstorm words that describe different weather conditions, noting the form of water in each case. Have students use words to compare the temperature inside the classroom with the temperature outside. Review the *water cycle* and write key vocabulary words on the board for students to learn and practice saying. (For example, *solid*, *liquid*, *gas*, *precipitation*, *evaporation*, *condensation*, *temperature*, and *thermometer*.) Have students draw pictures of different weather conditions.

Apply

Write the sentences from the following chart on the board or on large poster paper. Have students take turns echoing or reading one line at a time and identifying key vocabulary words. Then have students work with partners to make up sentences using those words.

The Water Cycle Goes On and On and On

Not all water is a wet liquid. Some water is solid, such as ice.

The heat from sunlight warms water, and it becomes a gas called water vapor.

Water vapor condenses in clouds.

Rain or other precipitation falls from the clouds.

This water goes back to Earth's surface.

Then the water cycle begins again.

Lesson 1 — Where Is Water Found on Earth?

① Build Background

Access Prior Knowledge

When to Use	Proficiency Levels
Before introducing the lesson 🕐 15 minutes	✔ Beginning ✔ Intermediate ✔ Advanced

Explain what a riddle is, then pose the following: You use it every day. Without it, you would die. It is wet. It is as important as the air around you. What is it? *(water)* Ask students why they think water is important. List their reasons. Point out that water covers three-fourths of Earth. Draw a circle on the board, then shade three quarters. Explain how to read a pie or circle graph and review such words as *graph*, *circle*, and *quarter*.

Preteach Lesson Vocabulary

fresh water, glacier, groundwater

List the vocabulary words on the board.

Have students look in the lesson to find the vocabulary words.

- Write the word *fresh* on the board and explain that *fresh* has many meanings. For example, We baked a *fresh* batch of cookies (newly done, made, or gathered); Pat moved to South America to get a *fresh* start in life (new; another); We stepped outside the hot room to get a breath of *fresh* air (clean or refreshing); She stayed after school for being *fresh* to the teacher (rude, disrespectful). In this lesson, *fresh* means "not salty." A lake has *fresh* water.

- Tell students that a *glacier* is a huge sheet of ice. Write the word *glacier* and have students note its pronunciation (GLA-shuhr).

- Discuss that in some areas of Earth, people dig wells to bring *groundwater* up from the ground.

Build Fluency

Pair students and have them ask each other questions about water. Or you may ask the class questions about water in round-robin fashion. Some questions might be the following: *How do you use water? From where do you get water? What is a water fountain? What is a faucet? How can you keep water cold? What happens when you put water in a freezer? About how much water do you use in a day? Why is it important to save water?*

© Harcourt

② Scaffold the Content

Preview the Lesson

- Ask students to point to the title of the lesson as you read it aloud. Explain that they will find the answer to this question in the lesson.
- As you look through the photographs, captions, and subheads of the lesson with students, help them understand that water is important to living things, and to Earth's environment. Water is found on Earth in many forms—fresh water, salt water, and frozen water.

Investigate, p. 305

Before students begin the Investigate:

- Discuss the meaning of words students will need to know in order to do this activity: *globe, index finger, toss, catch, data* (information), *recorder* (one who records, or writes), *estimate* (make a reasonable guess).
- Divide the class into groups, review the procedure with them, have them gather and record data and come to their own conclusions. When students are done, ask whether their estimates came close to the actual fact that three-quarters of Earth's surface is covered by water.

Modify Instruction—Multilevel Strategies

Background/Experience Discuss the difference between fresh water and salt water. Explain that most of Earth's water is salt water. Have students look at a globe as you call their attention to the three major salt-water bodies that surround the United States: the Atlantic Ocean, the Pacific Ocean, and the Gulf of Mexico. If a map of the United States is available, have students locate these three bodies of water. Ask students to name other bodies of salt water they may be familiar with around the world.

Beginning Have students think of water's importance in their lives. Call on volunteers to pantomime ways in which they use water *(to water plants, to shower, to brush teeth, to drink, to wash a car or pet, to swim or bathe in).*

Intermediate Have students brainstorm the names of organisms that live in the oceans and write the names on the board. Have students draw a picture that illustrates some of the underwater life identified. Students should label each of the organisms in their drawings.

Advanced Have students write a paragraph describing one way they use water or why it is important to save water.

© Harcourt

For All Students Draw a word web on the board as students brainstorm words that come to mind when they think of water, such as *wet, thirsty, ice, frozen, damp, moist,* or *rainy.*

Extend

Have students complete the **Show What You Know** activity on page 123 to demonstrate their understanding of Earth's water.

③ Apply and Assess

At Home in the Water

When to Use	Proficiency Levels
With Reading Review p. 311 🕐 20 minutes	✔ Beginning ✔ Intermediate ✔ Advanced

- Invite students to think of all the plants and animals that live in water and to compile a list of them. Then have pairs of students talk about the plants and animals that were mentioned.

- Make a two-column chart on the board with the headings *Fresh Water* and *Salt Water.* As a group, decide whether each plant or animal from the list lives in salt water or fresh water. Volunteers may then write the names of the organisms in the appropriate columns of the chart.

Informal Assessment

Beginning	Intermediate	Advanced
Have students look at a map or globe and point to the landforms and the different bodies of water. Explain that water nearly always appears blue on a map, but different colors may be used to distinguish different landforms (mountains, for example). Invite students to make up sentences using the word *water* in each. *(Answers will vary.)*	Have students think of what they have learned in this lesson and write a word to complete each of the following sentences. Most of Earth is covered by salt _____. Water that collects under the ground is called _____. Fresh water lakes do not contain _____. *(Answers: water; groundwater; salt)*	Ask students to write a paragraph telling where they would travel to find fresh water, frozen fresh water, or salt water. What are some things they might do there? *(Answers will vary. Examples: take pictures, go boating, go swimming)*

Name _____

Date _____

Water, Water Everywhere!

Some of Earth's water is fresh water. Some of Earth's water is salt water.
Some water is frozen. Write each word from the word box in the correct
place in the chart below.

Atlantic Ocean	**Mississippi River**	**glacier**
Gulf of Mexico	**Rio Grande**	
Lake Michigan	**Pacific Ocean**	

Fresh	Salt	Frozen

School-Home Connection: Have students take this page home to share with
family members. They can tell what they have learned about Earth's water.

2 What Is the Water Cycle?

① Build Background

Access Prior Knowledge

When to Use	Proficiency Levels
Before introducing the lesson	✔ Beginning
⏱ 15 minutes	✔ Intermediate
	✔ Advanced

Write the word *liquid* on the board and ask students to tell what they know about liquids. List phrases or draw sketches on the board to summarize that knowledge. Ask volunteers to name examples of liquids and list them. Repeat the activity for *solid* and then for *gas*.

Preteach Lesson Vocabulary

condensation, evaporation, precipitation, water cycle

List the vocabulary words on the board.

Have students look through the lesson to find the vocabulary words.

- Tell students that clues to understanding vocabulary words are often found by reading the words just before or after the boldface word. Read the words that surround *condensation* and *evaporation*. Repeat for *precipitation* and *water cycle*.

- Explain that *evaporation* has to do with heat. Water must gain heat for it to evaporate. Help students understand that *condensation* is the opposite of *evaporation*. When water vapor *loses* heat, the gas becomes liquid. The process of a gas turning into liquid is *condensation*.

- Explain to students that *precipitation* refers to rain, snow, sleet, and hail.

- In discussing the *water cycle*, be sure that students understand that without the Sun, there would be no water cycle.

Build Fluency

Have students read the following statements with you, and then have them say the vocabulary word that fits. Have students say each word as they clap out the syllables.

When gas turns into a liquid, this is called _____. *(condensation)*

When water heats up and changes to water vapor, this is called _____. *(evaporation)*

When water in clouds falls to Earth, the result is _____. *(precipitation)*

② Scaffold the Content

Preview the Lesson

Ask students to point to the lesson title as you read it aloud. Explain that the answer to this question can be found in the lesson. Students may scan the section headings to preview the location of the answer.

- Refer students to the picture and the Fast Fact on this same page. Allow time for students to tell what they know about dinosaurs and when they lived.
- Continue to look through the lesson with students, having them understand that water changes forms and moves from place to place in a never-ending cycle.

Investigate, p. 313

Before students begin the Investigate:

- Define a *terrarium* as a container where plants can be grown.
- Divide students into small groups. If students have difficulty understanding the directions, refer them to the photograph showing the activity, or demonstrate how to set up and use the equipment before the groups begin work.
- Remind students that *infer* means "to draw a conclusion based on data or on first-hand observations."

Modify Instruction—Multilevel Strategies

Background/Experience Draw or share pictures of a teakettle with water boiling, a glass of drinking water, and an ice cube. Tell students that the pictures are examples of the three forms of water. Explain that all water on Earth is in one of these states—liquid, solid, or gas. Solid water is ice. The water in a glass is liquid. Water in gas form cannot be seen. It is called *water vapor*. Point to the space just above the teakettle's whistle, where there is no "steam." This is where water is in the gaseous state. The little cloud that everyone calls "steam" is really condensed water—a liquid. Have students point to each example and identify its state (solid, liquid, gas). Explain that water changes when it gains or loses heat.

Beginning Have students tell something about each example pictured and identify it as a solid, liquid, or gaseous form of water.

Intermediate Have students explain how water changes form when it is heated and when it cools. Have students say what happens when a pot of water is left cooking on the stove. Ask what causes water to turn to ice?

© Harcourt

Advanced Have students suppose that they place a glass of water outdoors on a very hot day. Have them write what they think would happen to the water. Then have them suppose that the temperature outdoors is below freezing. Tell them to write what they think would happen to the water.

For All Students Have students tell which form of water to expect at the following temperatures: 30°F, 60°F, and 212°F. As a group, discuss the water cycle, including the terms *condensation*, *evaporation*, *precipitation*, and *water cycle*.

Extend

Have students complete the **Show What You Know** activity on page 127 to demonstrate their understanding of the water cycle.

③ Apply and Assess

Forms of Water

When to Use With Reading Review p. 319 20 minutes	Proficiency Levels ✔ Beginning ✔ Intermediate ✔ Advanced

Materials: old magazines, scissors, paper, tape

- Have students work in groups to cut out magazine pictures that show or suggest water in its three forms. For example, a picture of a freezer would suggest ice, the solid form of water; a picture of a pot of boiling water would suggest the gaseous form of water; a picture of a bottle of water would suggest the liquid form of water.

- Direct students to organize their pictures on three sheets of paper, one sheet for each form of water.

- Ask the groups to label the sheets of paper *Solids*, *Liquids*, or *Gases*. Then have volunteers from each group show the pictures to the class, identify each item, and tell what form of water it represents.

Informal Assessment

Beginning	Intermediate	Advanced
Have students look outside to see if they can spot any clouds. Invite students to tell what happens when the tiny water drops in clouds become too heavy. *(Answer: When the drops become too big and heavy, they fall as rain or some other kind of precipitation.)*	Have students think of what they have learned in this lesson and say the vocabulary word that names what is happening in each of the following sentences. "Water that is boiling in a teakettle changes to water vapor. The gas form of water is in the air. Temperature drops at night and we see dew on leaves in the morning." *(Answers: evaporation; water vapor; condensation)*	Ask students to write the form of water that describes each kind of precipitation: rain, snow, sleet, and hail. *(Answers: rain is liquid water; snow and hail are ice; sleet is partly frozen rain)*

The Water Cycle

Use the words from the word box to label each step of the water cycle. Then draw arrows to show the order of the water cycle.

precipitation	evaporation	condensation

The sun shines on lakes, streams, oceans, rivers, and land. The heat from sunlight causes water to change to water vapor. The water vapor rises into the air.

_____

The water in clouds falls back to Earth on lakes, streams, oceans, rivers, and land as rain, sleet, snow, or hail.

_____

Water vapor in the air cools and changes back to water. The water collects on tiny dust particles and forms clouds.

_____

School-Home Connection: Have students take this page home to share with family members. They can use this page to explain the water cycle.

Lesson 3

What Is Weather?

① Build Background

Access Prior Knowledge

When to Use	Proficiency Levels
Before introducing the lesson 15 minutes	✔ Beginning ✔ Intermediate ✔ Advanced

Write the words *hot, sunny, cloudy, warm, cold, rainy,* and *snow* on the board. Review each word's pronunciation, and meaning. Then ask what all the words have in common. Have students think of other words that relate to weather. Explain that weather is what is happening in the air (atmosphere) at a certain place and time. Discuss what the weather is like where students live now. What is the weather like in their home countries?

Preteach Lesson Vocabulary

atmosphere, oxygen, weather, temperature, thermometer

Materials: thermometer

List the vocabulary words on the board.

Have students look through the lesson to find the vocabulary words.

- Display a thermometer. Have students identify it and practice saying the word. Ask how many syllables they hear when you clap out the word. Ask students to tell what a thermometer is used for. Allow students to share experiences they've had with thermometers when they were ill and had a fever.

- Write the word *anemometer* next to the word *thermometer* and have students point to the letters that are the same. Explain that an *anemometer* measures wind speed; a thermometer measures how hot or cold something is.

- Point out that students can't hold, taste, or see *air* because air is a *gas*. It contains *oxygen*, the gas we need to live. Remind students that air also contains other gases besides oxygen.

Build Fluency

Point out that weather changes from day to day. Have students discuss the weather today and compare it to yesterday's weather. If possible, look at today's newspaper and ask students to discuss the weather prediction for tomorrow. Allow students to talk about the things they do in different kinds of weather and to tell the kind of weather they most prefer.

© Harcourt

② Scaffold the Content

Preview the Lesson

- Discuss the difference between the homophones *whether* and *weather*.
- On the same page, have students note how a weather vane shows wind *direction.*
- Ask for examples of how weather is helpful to people and examples of how weather is harmful to people.
- Look through the lesson with students, helping them to understand that many instruments are used to collect data at weather stations so that weather predictions may be made. Discuss which people might especially need to know about what the weather will be like *(people planning outdoor activities, people who work outside, farmers, and so on)*.

Investigate, p. 321

Before students begin the Investigate:

- Make sure students understand the meanings of such words and phrases as *half-full, one-fourth*, and *seal*. Point out that *seal* has multiple meanings and discuss its meaning here.
- Divide the class into groups and use the photos as you walk students through the steps of the activity. Demonstrate any steps, as necessary.

Modify Instruction—Multilevel Strategies

Background/Experience

Materials: thermometer

Have students guess the temperature outside the school and the temperature of the classroom. How do they think the temperature outside compares with the temperature inside? If possible, use a thermometer to measure each temperature. Ask what other instruments weather forecasters use to learn what the weather is like (i.e., *anemometer* to measure wind speed, computer, barometer, rain gauge, and so on).

Beginning Have students draw pictures of the different kinds of weather they've experienced and label each one with words such as *rainy, snowy, foggy*, and *hot*. Call on volunteers to tell about their pictures and to respond to simple questions.

Intermediate Have students describe the day's weather and predict what the weather will be for the next few days. Ask how clouds are usually good predictors of weather.

Advanced Have students write a paragraph describing ways in which weather can be helpful to people, plants, and animals. Then have them write a paragraph describing ways in which severe weather can be harmful to people, plants, animals, buildings, and so on.

For All Students Draw a "Weather Watch" word web on the board and have students brainstorm words used to describe weather, such as *breezy*, *snowy*, *windy*, *cold*, *wet*, and *humid*.

Extend

Have students complete the **Show What You Know** activity on page 131 to demonstrate their understanding of weather.

③ Apply and Assess

What's the Weather?

When to Use	Proficiency Levels
With Reading Review p. 327	✔ Beginning
🕐 20 minutes	✔ Intermediate
	✔ Advanced

- Invite students to think of the importance of weather forecasts.
- Ask volunteers to describe a TV weather forecast. What does the forecaster show on the weather map? What symbols are used? Share a weather map from a newspaper for students to examine.
- Have small groups work together to devise a poster-board weather map for the country that uses various weather symbols.
- Volunteers may then present a mock weather broadcast for the Northeast, South, Midwest, Southwest, and Northwest. Encourage students to use as many weather words as possible in the weather forecast.

Informal Assessment

Beginning	Intermediate	Advanced
Have a pair of students think of a "weather riddle." Ask students to include three clues to help describe a kind of weather. Have the rest of the class guess the weather being described. An example of a weather riddle for rain might be: You carry an umbrella. You see puddles. Everything gets wet. *(Answers will vary.)*	Have students tell two examples of weather that are beneficial. Then have them tell two examples of weather that are harmful. *(Answers will wary.)*	Ask students to write about a weather instrument and what the instrument measures. *(Answers will vary.)*

© Harcourt

Weather Words

Write the weather words from the word box in the correct place on
the chart below.

snow	rain	wind

_____	_____	_____
blowing leaves	snowman	umbrella
tornado	blizzard	flooding
hurricane	very cold	wet

School-Home Connection: Have students take this page home to share with
family members. They can tell what they have learned about weather.

© Harcourt

10 Earth's Place in the Solar System

Develop Scientific Concepts and Vocabulary

In this chapter, students will learn about Earth, the Moon, and the rest of the solar system, including the reason for the seasons, day and night, and eclipses. They will also be able to identify the nine planets in order from the Sun and compare and contrast the inner and outer planets.

Preview Scientific Principles

Walk through the chapter with students, pausing to read aloud or to have volunteers read aloud the three questions that are lesson titles. Encourage students to briefly discuss each question and to tell what they already know that might help them answer the questions.

When to Use With Chapter Opener	Proficiency Levels
🕐 25 minutes	✔ Beginning ✔ Intermediate ✔ Advanced

Lesson 1: What Causes Earth's Seasons?

- Show students a variety of clothing worn during different seasons.
- Have them discuss the time of year they would wear each type of clothing, using the names of the seasons in their sentences.
- Ask students to tell what they know about the reason for the change of seasons.

Lesson 2: How Do Earth and the Moon Interact?

- Ask students to describe what they see in the night sky, including the Moon.
- Have students draw pictures of what the Moon looks like at different times of the month.
- Discuss the pictures and point out that the Moon does not always look the same. Ask students to talk about what they know about the reasons for these changes.

© Harcourt

Lesson 3: What Is the Solar System?

- Show students a picture of the planets in our solar system. Ask if they know what the image shows.
- Invite a volunteer to count the planets shown in the picture. Then have the students count the planets together.
- Ask volunteers to describe each planet.

Practice

Write the vocabulary words from the chapter on the board. Read through the words with students and help them to spell, pronounce, and understand each term. Then help students create a picture dictionary for them to use as they work through each lesson. Invite students to use images from the chapter to help them create drawings or provide magazines from which they can cut images. Give students an opportunity to read through their dictionaries with a partner telling their definitions and showing the pictures they included.

Apply

Write the sentences from the following chart on the board and have students take turns echoing or reading a line aloud. Remind students that *revolve* means to circle around. Invite a volunteer to act as the Sun. Have other volunteers act out the motion of the planets *revolving* around the Sun. Invite students to draw the path of a planet revolving around the Sun.

Solar System Movements

The Sun is at the center of our solar system.
The Earth revolves around the Sun.
Mercury revolves around the Sun.
Venus revolves around the Sun.
Mars revolves around the Sun.
Jupiter revolves around the Sun.
Saturn revolves around the Sun.
Uranus revolves around the Sun.
Neptune revolves around the Sun.
Pluto revolves around the Sun, too.

What Causes Earth's Seasons?

① Build Background

Access Prior Knowledge

When to Use	Proficiency Levels
Before introducing the lesson	✔ Beginning
⏱ 15 minutes	✔ Intermediate
	Advanced

Materials: pictures showing the four seasons

Show pictures that represent each season, possibly using a picture of the same location during the four seasons. Ask students to describe each picture. Be sure students point out changes, such as color, leaves, and clothing worn by people in the picture. Tell students that these pictures show the different seasons, or times of year. Ask students to name the seasons, or name each season for them as they repeat.

Preteach Lesson Vocabulary

axis, rotation, revolution

Materials: masking tape

List the vocabulary words on the board.

- Have students turn to page 338. Point out the image of Earth's axis. Point to the representational line for the axis and say *axis*. Have students repeat as they point to the line. Explain that this line is not real, but it shows the way Earth spins, or *rotates*.

- Invite a volunteer to hold a finger to the top of his or her head. Have the student begin to spin slowly in place. Tell students that the volunteer is showing *rotation*, or spinning around an imaginary line. Explain that the finger points to the axis. Students can mimic this motion themselves.

- Have students find *revolution* on page 339. Bring a volunteer to the front of the class to act as the Sun. Mark a large circle of tape around the "sun." Then have a student act as Earth by walking along the tape. Explain that this motion models making a *revolution* around the Sun.

Build Fluency

Have partners or small groups discuss what they see, do, and wear during the different seasons. Have them use the following sentence frame for their conversation.

I see/do/wear _____ in the _____ (*name of season*).

© Harcourt

② Scaffold the Content

Preview the Lesson

- Have students preview the images that show rotation and revolution on pages 338 and 339. Invite students to use their fingers or small classroom objects to simulate each type of movement.
- Refer students to the pictures on pages 340–341. Allow time for them to describe the sunlight angles at different times during the year.
- Have students preview the title and images on page 342. Summarize that the page explains why Earth has day and night. Allow time for students to tell what they know about the reasons for the change. Clarify that Earth's rotation is responsible.

Investigate, p. 337

Materials: graph paper

- Before students begin the Investigate, review the use of graph paper. Write *graph paper* on the board and point out a sample to students.
- Model how to draw a circle on graph paper and count the squares inside it.
- Allow time for partners to draw their own circles, trade papers, and count the squares inside each other's circles.
- Explain that students will use this skill in steps 1 and 2 of the Investigate.

Modify Instruction—Multilevel Strategies

Language and Vocabulary Students may have difficulty understanding the difference between *rotate* and *revolve*. Use the following activities to help clarify the meaning of each word, and relate the root words with their extended forms in the words *rotation* and *revolution*.

Beginning Play a modified version of "Simon Says." Have a volunteer lead the class and say *rotate* or *revolve*. The class then models the appropriate motion. Repeat with new volunteer leaders.

Intermediate Provide pairs of students with two balls and index cards with the terms *rotate* and *revolve*. Partners take turns choosing a card and using the balls to model the motion. They should explain what they are doing to the partner as they move the balls.

© Harcourt

Advanced Have students choose classroom objects to model rotation and revolution. Direct them to show their models to the class and explain what they are doing. Their explanations should include definitions of *rotation* and *revolution*.

For All Students Help students use modeling clay to build models of rotation and revolution. They can modify or expand their models as they work through the lesson.

Extend

Have students complete the **Show What You Know** activity on page 137 to demonstrate their understanding of rotation and revolution.

③ Apply and Assess

Make Word Form Charts

When to Use With Reading Review p. 343 ⏱ 20 minutes	Proficiency Levels ✔ Beginning ✔ Intermediate ✔ Advanced

Materials: chart paper, markers

- Have students work in small groups to make charts showing different forms of the words *rotate* and *revolve*.

- On the board, help students to list different forms of the word *rotate*, such as *rotates*, *rotating*, *rotated*, and *rotation*. Do the same for *revolve*.

- Using a different piece of chart paper for each word, have students copy the words from the board. Then have them work as a group to write a sentence for each word. Encourage them to draw an illustration to go with each of their sentences.

- Invite groups to share their sentences and illustrations with the class.

Informal Assessment

Beginning	Intermediate	Advanced
Have students use their bodies to show the meaning of *rotate*. Then invite them to show a *revolution* around their chair. *(Answer: Students should demonstrate* rotate *by spinning their bodies in a circle. They should make one complete turn around their chair to demonstrate* revolve.*)*	Have students complete the following sentence frames to demonstrate their understanding of *rotate* and *revolve*: Earth _____ on its axis. Earth _____ around the Sun. *(Answers; rotates; revolves)*	Have students write sentences to describe the way Earth moves around its axis and the way it moves around the Sun. Encourage them to use the terms *rotate* and *revolve* in their sentences. *(Possible answers: Earth rotates around its axis in about 24 hours. Earth revolves around the Sun in one year.)*

Draw the Earth's Movement

In the first box, draw and label a picture showing Earth's rotation.
In the second box, draw and label a picture showing Earth's revolution
around the Sun. Use arrows to show how Earth moves in each picture.

School-Home Connection: Have students take this page home to share with
family members. They can use this page to tell about Earth's rotation and revolution.

Lesson 2 How Do Earth and the Moon Interact?

1 Build Background

Access Prior Knowledge

When to Use	Proficiency Levels
Before introducing the lesson 15 minutes	✔ Beginning ✔ Intermediate Advanced

Materials: picture of the Moon

Show students a picture of the Moon. Say "Moon" as you point to it and ask students to repeat it. Ask students when and where they see the Moon. Ask them to describe it and tell if the Moon always looks the same. Invite volunteers to come to the board and draw the Moon in the different ways they have seen it in the sky.

Preteach Lesson Vocabulary

> **phase, lunar cycle, lunar eclipse, solar eclipse**

List the vocabulary words on the board.

- Write *phase* on the board. Say the term as you run your fingers under the word. Underline the letters *ph*. Tell students that these letters together make the /f/ sound. Have students repeat the word. Then refer them to the drawings they made of the different shapes of the Moon. Explain that these shapes are the *phases* of the Moon.

- Then point out the next two vocabulary terms and the term *lunar* in each one. Relate this word to the Spanish *luna*, which means "moon."

- Explain that a *cycle* is a pattern that keeps repeating, so a *lunar cycle* is a moon pattern that repeats. The lunar cycle is the repeating pattern of the phases.

- Explain that an *eclipse* happens when a space object casts a shadow on another object. Connect *lunar eclipse* to the idea that a shadow makes the Moon dark.

- Point out that *solar* comes from the word *sol*, meaning "sun," so a solar eclipse means a shadow makes the Sun dark.

Build Fluency

Have students work with a partner. Refer them to the pictures of the phases of the Moon on pages 346 and 347. Have partners take turns pointing to a phase and the other saying the name of the phase using this sentence frame:

That is the _____ phase of the Moon.

© Harcourt

② **Scaffold the Content**

When to Use With pp. 344–350	Proficiency Levels
⏱ 20 minutes	✔ Beginning ✔ Intermediate ✔ Advanced

Preview the Lesson

Refer students to page 344. Invite them to pick out and define any words they know in the title and describe what they see in the picture.

- Connect the images on pages 346 and 347 to the phases of the Moon. Explain that it takes about 28 days for the Moon to make one complete revolution around Earth.
- Have students preview the pictures of lunar and solar eclipses and tell how they are the same and different. Remind students that shadows happen when light is blocked. Help them to understand that eclipses involve shadows made by space objects.

Investigate, p. 345

- Before students begin the Investigate, preview the steps by modeling them with students. Walk them through each step so they are clear about where to stand and what to do.
- Point to each member of the group and name what they represent; for example, that the flashlight is the Sun and the ball is the Moon.

Modify Instruction—Multilevel Strategies

Language and Vocabulary The adjectives *lunar* and *solar* can distinguish between different kinds of eclipses and identify other types of space phenomena. Use these activities to help students distinguish between the terms. Write the words *lunar* and *solar* on the board. Invite students to repeat the words and practice writing them. Review that *lunar* comes from *luna*, meaning "moon," and *solar* comes from *sol*, meaning "sun."

Beginning Show students a picture of the Sun and a picture of the Moon. Have them label each one appropriately with *lunar* or *solar*.

Intermediate Have students use sentences to explain the meanings of *lunar* and *solar*.

Advanced Have students write sentences to define *lunar* and *solar*.

For All Students Have students draw and label diagrams of lunar and solar eclipses, using the terms *lunar* and *solar* in the diagrams or in titles. Students can update, correct, or improve the diagrams as they work though the lesson.

Have students complete the **Show What You Know** activity on page 141 to demonstrate their understanding of the terms *lunar* and *solar*.

③ Apply and Assess

Solar and Lunar Mural

When to Use	Proficiency Levels
With Reading Review p. 351	✔ Beginning
⏱ 25 minutes	✔ Intermediate
	✔ Advanced

Materials: butcher paper, drawing paper, magazines, scissors, glue, markers

- Have students work in small groups.
- Have them divide a piece of butcher paper in half and label one side *lunar* and the second side *solar*.
- Direct them to draw or find pictures that relate to the Sun and the Moon. Then have them paste those images on the appropriate sides of the butcher paper.
- Encourage students to write words or phrases related to the Sun or Moon on the corresponding sides as well. Students may also wish to write captions for the pictures.
- Invite students to present and talk about their posters. They should tell what the images are and how they relate to *lunar* or *solar*.

Informal Assessment

Beginning	Intermediate	Advanced
Show students a picture of the Sun and of the Moon. Say *solar*. Have students repeat and point to the picture that relates to the term. Do the same with *lunar*. *(Answer: Students should be able to correctly identify that* solar *is related to the Sun and that* lunar *is related to the Moon.)*	Have students draw a picture to demonstrate *lunar* and one for *solar*. *(Answers will vary.)*	Have students write two sentences. In the first sentence, have them correctly use the word *solar*. In the second sentence, have them correctly use the word *lunar*. *(Answers will vary but should show an understanding that the word* solar *is related to the Sun, and the word* lunar *is related to the Moon.)*

Name _____

Date _____

Words About the Sun and Moon

Write each term from the word box in the column where it belongs. Then write a sentence using one of the terms from the word box.

| lunar cycle | lunar landing | solar power |
| lunar eclipse | solar eclipse | solar rays |

Sun	Moon

_____

_____

_____

School-Home Connection: Have students take this page home to share with family members. They can use it to tell what they know about the words *solar* and *lunar*.

What Is the Solar System?

① Build Background

Access Prior Knowledge

When to Use	Proficiency Levels
Before introducing the lesson ⏱ 15 minutes	✔ Beginning ✔ Intermediate Advanced

Materials: globe

- Show students a globe. Tell them that a globe shows what Earth looks like. Ask students to tell what they know about Earth. Tell students that Earth is one of the objects in our solar system.
- Have students name other objects in the solar system, such as the planets, the Moon, or the Sun, and tell what they know about them.

Preteach Lesson Vocabulary

planet, orbit, solar system, star, constellation

Materials: globe, picture of the sun

List the vocabulary words on the board.

- Write *solar system* on the board and circle the word *solar*. Remind students that this word means "related to the Sun." Explain that the *solar system* includes all of the objects that revolve around the Sun. Allow time for students to identify objects in the solar system and explain in their own words why they belong. Guide students to the understanding that planets and moons are in the solar system because they revolve around the Sun.
- Explain that Earth is a *planet* and there are nine planets in the solar system.
- Show students a picture of the Sun. Tell them that the Sun is a *star*, or large ball of burning gases.
- Ask students if they have ever seen any other stars. Tell them that there are millions of stars in the sky, but they are farther away from Earth than the Sun. Point out that we see the stars in the sky in patterns called *constellations*.

Build Fluency

Write the names of the nine planets on the board. Read through them with students. Then have them work with a partner and take turns using each planet in the following sentence frame:

_____ is a planet.

© Harcourt

② Scaffold the Content

Preview the Lesson

When to Use	Proficiency Levels
With pp. 352–360	✔ Beginning
20 minutes	✔ Intermediate
	✔ Advanced

- Read the title on page 352. Have students describe what they see in the picture, and allow time for them to tell what they know about any objects they recognize.
- Refer students to the pictures of the planets on pages 354 and 355. Remind them that there are nine planets in our solar system. Invite them to point to each planet and repeat the names as you read them.
- Have students find page 355 and identify that the Sun is an object in the solar system.
- Have students scan the section titles on pages 356 to 359 to identify which planets are inner planets and which are outer planets.

Investigate, p. 353

- Before beginning the Investigate, clarify with students the meaning of the words *closest*, *farthest*, and *in between*.
- Invite three volunteers to come to the front of the room. Position them so that one student is closest to the door, a second is in between, and a third is farthest from the door.
- Ask volunteers to describe each student's location relative to the door with statements such as *(student name) is closest to the door*.

Modify Instruction—Multilevel Strategies

Language and Vocabulary Students will benefit from additional exposure to the planetary names. Help them learn the names of the planets and distinguish between the inner and outer planets with these activities.

Display a picture or model of the solar system using different sizes of circles or balls. Name each planet in the drawing or model.

Beginning Read the names of the planets in order several times with students. Ask them to work together in small groups to name the nine planets in order.

Intermediate Point to a specific planet. Ask students to name it and classify it as either an *inner* or *outer* planet.

Advanced Ask students to write the names of the nine planets in order and label each one as an inner or outer planet.

For All Students Have students write the names of the nine planets on separate index cards and put as many of the cards in order as they can. Students can update or correct the order of the cards as they work through the lesson.

Extend

Have students complete the **Show What You Know** activity on page 145 to demonstrate their understanding of the solar system.

③ Apply and Assess

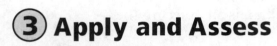

When to Use	Proficiency Levels
With Reading Review p. 361 20 minutes	✔ Beginning ✔ Intermediate ✔ Advanced

Place Your Planets

Materials: butcher paper, construction paper, markers, tape

- Have students make a model of the solar system on butcher paper. Direct them to draw the Sun in the center of the paper. Have them draw nine circles to show the planets' orbits, but not the planets.
- Have students cut out and label circles to represent the nine planets.
- Then, one at a time, invite students to tape their planets on the appropriate orbit path on the model.
- Have students use the model to discuss the relative location of each planet to the Sun and to Earth.

Informal Assessment

Beginning	Intermediate	Advanced
Show students a model or drawing of the solar system. Ask them to point to the inner planets. Then have them point to the outer planets. *(Answers: Students should indicate Mercury, Venus, Earth, and Mars as the inner planets. They should point to Jupiter, Saturn, Uranus, Neptune, and Pluto as the outer planets.)*	Point to a planet and have students say the name. Then ask if the planet is an inner or outer planet. *(Answers: Students should accurately identify each planet and correctly classify it as either inner or outer.)*	Have students copy and complete the following sentences: The nine planets are _____, _____, _____, _____, _____, _____, _____, _____, and _____. Earth is the _____ planet from the Sun. *(Answers; Mercury, Venus, Earth, Mars, Jupiter, Saturn, Uranus, Neptune, and Pluto; third)*

Name _____

Date _____

The Order of Planets

Write the names of the planets in order from the Sun. Then list the inner planets and outer planets in the table.

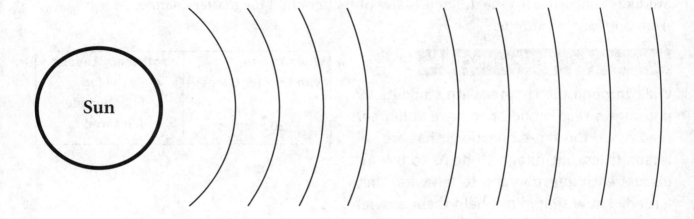

Inner Planets	Outer Planets

School-Home Connection: Have students take this page home to share with family members. They can use this page to tell about the solar system.

© Harcourt

11 Properties of Matter

Develop Scientific Concepts and Vocabulary

In this chapter, students will identify matter and describe its physical properties. Students will also learn the different states of matter and how matter changes from one form to another.

Preview Scientific Principles

Walk through the chapter with students, pausing to read aloud or to have volunteers read aloud the three questions that are lesson titles. Encourage students to briefly discuss each question and to tell what they already know that might help them answer the questions.

When to Use With Chapter Opener	Proficiency Levels
⏱ 20 minutes	✔ Beginning ✔ Intermediate ✔ Advanced

Lesson 1: What Is Matter?

- Have students close their eyes and lift a book. Allow time for them to feel the book. Ask volunteers to describe it—possibly as hard, smooth, heavy, and large.

- Explain that the book is a type of *matter*, or anything that takes up space. Ask students to identify other examples of matter—shoes, trees, and air—and justify their choices. Ask them to name things that are *not* matter—ideas, feelings, or heat.

Lesson 2: What Are States of Matter?

- Ask students to describe the properties of water and ice, and compare them. Ask volunteers to explain how water can turn into ice and how ice can turn into water.

- Explain that ice and water are different *states* of the same kind of matter.

- Say that ice is a *solid*, water is a *liquid*, and steam is a *gas*. Ask students to describe each state and to tell what they know about solids, liquids, and gases.

Lesson 3: How Does Matter Change?

- Give students a sheet of paper. Have them use their senses to observe and describe it.

- Then, direct students to crumple the paper and compare it to the flat sheet. Discuss whether the paper is still paper or whether it has become something else.

© Harcourt

- Summarize that the crumpled paper has different properties, but it is still paper. Explain that these kinds of changes are called *physical changes*.

Practice

Write *MATTER* on the board. Encourage students to look around the classroom and outside the windows to dictate a list of examples, such as air, flag, pencils, or water. Then help students sort the list into three categories—solid, liquid, and gas. Encourage students to use phrases or sentences to explain why they sorted each example into the category they chose.

Apply

Write the poem from the following chart on the board, including the bracketed words in the second stanza. Read the poem aloud with students or have them echo read it with you. After they practice reading the poem, erase the words *dirt*, *rocks*, and *hair* so that students can insert their own words in the poem. Have them read the poem aloud with their own words.

Matter, Matter, All Around

How do you know what matter is?
"Easy," you say with a smile on your face.
Matter is anything that takes up space.

Matter is water and trees and air.
Matter is books and ice and glue.
Matter is _____ [dirt] and
_____ [rocks] and _____ [hair].
Matter is me and matter is you.

Lesson 1 — What Is Matter?

1 Build Background

Access Prior Knowledge

<table>
<tr><td>When to Use
Before introducing the lesson
 20 minutes</td><td>Proficiency Levels
✔ Beginning
✔ Intermediate
Advanced</td></tr>
</table>

Give students an opportunity to identify things that surround them, such as books, pencils, plants, and themselves. Have them use familiar words to describe the objects and living things they identify. Encourage students to describe air, even though it cannot be seen.

Preteach Lesson Vocabulary

> **matter, physical property, mass, volume, density**

List the vocabulary words on the board.

- Remind students that *matter* has a number of meanings, as in the expression "What's the matter?" Discuss the meaning of that question as "What's the problem?" or "What's wrong?" Point out that *matter* has a different meaning in science.

- Have students find the vocabulary words on pages 374–379.

- Ask for a volunteer to hold up a book. Point to the book and review that it is a type of *matter* because it takes up space. Explain that anything that takes up space is matter. Ask students to name other things that take up space.

- Encourage students to describe the book's color, size, shape, and texture. Explain that color, size, shape, and texture are *physical properties*. Offer synonyms of *property*, such as trait, characteristic, or feature.

- Explain that two other physical properties are *mass* and *volume*. Define *mass* as the amount of matter in an object and *volume* as the amount of space an object takes up.

Build Fluency

Have students complete and read sentences like the ones below to identify some physical properties of classroom objects.

This pencil is _____.   That notebook is _____.   The student is _____.

The water is _____.   The rug is _____.   The air is _____.

© Harcourt

② Scaffold the Content

Preview the Lesson

When to Use With pp. 372–380	Proficiency Levels
🕐 20 minutes	✔ Beginning ✔ Intermediate ✔ Advanced

- Ask students to point to the title on page 372 as you read it aloud. Explain that after students complete the lesson, they should be able to define *matter*.

- Have students observe the picture. Ask volunteers to identify the different examples of matter in the picture. Possible answers may be the pitcher, the lemonade, the woman, the clothes she is wearing, and air. Have students tell why they think the objects they identify are matter.

- Ask students to identify other examples of matter shown throughout the lesson. Ask them to describe a physical property for each example they name.

Investigate, p. 373

- Before students begin the Investigate, display and demonstrate how to use a metric measuring cup.

- Allow time for partners to take turns measuring different amounts of water—including 100 mL—as they tell the partner what they are doing at each step.

Build comprehension and provide meaning for some of the other important technical words. Read aloud the words you choose, using each in a context sentence, and provide its meaning. Then, have students repeat the word and find it in their texts. *(mass,* p. 378; *volume,* p. 379; *density,* p. 379)*

Modify Instruction—Multilevel Strategies

Background/Experience Understanding the concept of matter, the focus of this lesson, involves understanding that matter is anything that takes up space. It also means being able to describe the physical properties of matter. The following exercises provide opportunities for students to describe those properties.

Beginning Have students draw a classroom object and write three words to describe its physical properties.

Intermediate Have students draw two classroom objects and write two phrases or sentences comparing their physical properties.

Advanced Have students draw three classroom objects. Direct them to write a sentence about each object, describing its physical properties. Then, have them write or say a sentence with the terms *matter* and *physical property* so that they define each term.

For All Students Have students make separate posters for air, water, and a doorknob. Have them list physical properties for each item on the poster. Ask them to add to the posters as they learn more about physical properties during the lesson.

Extend

Have the students complete the **Show What You Know** activity on page 151 to demonstrate their understanding of matter and its physical properties.

③ Apply and Assess

Sort Matter by Its Physical Properties

When to Use With Reading Review p. 381　🕐 15 minutes	Proficiency Levels ✔ Beginning ✔ Intermediate ✔ Advanced

Materials: ten small classroom objects and three boxes for each group

- Divide students into groups of four. Give each group 10 different classroom objects.
- Have students work together to sort the objects into three groups so that the objects share the same physical property. For example, all of the objects in one group may be red, the objects in the second group may have a smooth texture, and the objects in the third group may be shaped like balls.
- Have students put the groups of objects into the different boxes and label them with the shared physical property.
- Allow time for students to show how they sorted the objects and explain their sorting system.

Informal Assessment

Beginning	Intermediate	Advanced
Have each student pick a classroom object that is matter. *(Possible answers: pencil, book, desk, door)*	Have each student name one object that is matter and one that is not matter. *(Examples of matter include chair, rug, chalk, or air. Examples of nonmatter include heat, ideas, or feelings.)*	Have students select an object that is matter and use it to define the term. *(Matter is anything that takes up space.)*

© Harcourt

Physical Properties

Read the word in each diagram. Write a physical property in each of the
three boxes that describes the type of matter.

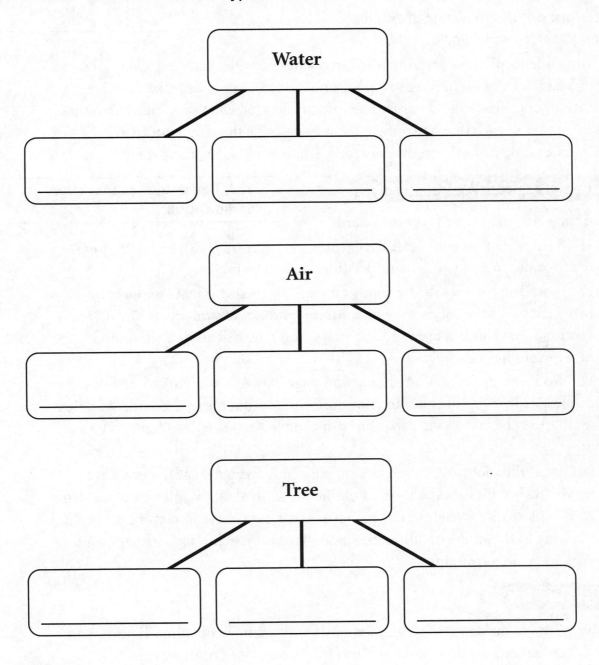

Water

Air

Tree

School-Home Connection: Have students take this page home to share
with family members. They can use this page to tell about matter and its
physical properties.

Lesson 2 What Are States of Matter?

① Build Background

Access Prior Knowledge

When to Use Before introducing the lesson 15 minutes	Proficiency Levels ✔ Beginning ✔ Intermediate Advanced

Materials: pictures showing the different states of water—solid, liquid, and gas

Show students pictures featuring the three states of water, such as a child ice skating on a lake, a child swimming in a pool, and a steaming pot or teakettle. Give students an opportunity to describe each picture and tell what they know about the state of matter in each one. Encourage them to describe the temperature in each state. Guide students to the terms *solid* for ice, *liquid* for water, and *gas* for steam.

Preteach Lesson Vocabulary

solid, liquid, gas, evaporation, condensation

List the vocabulary words on the board.

- Have students find the vocabulary words on pages 385–387 and help them practice the spelling and pronunciation of each term.
- Point out the pictures of the solids on page 385. Ask students to describe properties that the solids have in common and guide students to the understanding that solids have a specific shape and size. Ask students to name other examples of solids.
- Point out the pictures of the liquids on page 386. Ask students to describe properties that liquids have in common. Guide students to the understanding that liquids have a specific size, but can change shape. Ask students to name other examples of liquids.
- Point out the pictures of the gases on page 387. Explain that the gases are inside the bubbles and balloons. Remind students that air and steam are also gases. Ask students to describe properties that gases have in common. Guide students to the understanding that gases have no specific size or shape and expand to fill a container.

Build Fluency

Have partners make a set of 10 index cards with pictures of solids, liquids, and gases. They can cut out and paste pictures from magazines or draw their own pictures. Ask students to shuffle the cards and take turns flashing one to their partner. The partner should say "solid," "liquid," or "gas" to classify the object in the picture.

© Harcourt

152 ESL Support

② **Scaffold the Content**

When to Use	Proficiency Levels
With pp. 382–388	✔ Beginning
⏱ 20 minutes	✔ Intermediate
	✔ Advanced

Preview the Lesson

- Read the title on page 382. Tell students that they will learn to define *solid, liquid,* and *gas* and explain how these *states of matter* can change from one form to another.

- Explain that the word *states* refers to forms, types, or kinds. Remind students that ice, water, and steam are all types of water, but they exist in different forms or states.

- Refer students to page 388. Point out that the process of a liquid changing to a gas is called *evaporation*. The process of the gas changing back to a liquid is called *condensation*. Present a simple diagram or graphic organizer on the board to summarize these changes.

Investigate, p. 383

Materials: thermometers

- Before students begin the Investigate, review the terms *temperature* and *thermometer*. Explain that temperature tells how hot or cold something is. A thermometer is the tool that measures temperature.

- Display and model how to read a thermometer.

- Have partners take turns measuring the temperature in different parts of the room and telling each other what they are doing at every step. Encourage students to use the terms *temperature* and *thermometer*.

Modify Instruction—Multilevel Strategies

Background/Experience The following exercises help students practice using the terms *solid, liquid,* and *gas* and develop their understanding of the different states of matter.

    Beginning Have students write *solid, liquid,* and *gas* on separate index cards. Have them use the cards to label an appropriate classroom object in each category. Ask them to share and explain their choices with the group.

    Intermediate Have students write *solid, liquid,* and *gas* on separate index cards. Have them draw an example of the state of matter on the back of each card.

    Advanced Have students write *solid, liquid,* and *gas* on separate index cards. Have them write a definition for each term on the back of the cards.

    For All Students Help students make a word web for each of the states of matter. For each web, write *solid, liquid,* or *gas* in the center. Have students dictate or write words, phrases, or sentences that define or expand the meaning of the terms. Students can add to the word web as they work through the lesson.

© Harcourt

Have the students complete the **Show What You Know** activity on page 155 to demonstrate their understanding of the states of matter.

③ Apply and Assess

Make a Picture Web

When to Use	Proficiency Levels
With Reading Review p. 389 ⏱ 20 minutes	✔ Beginning ✔ Intermediate ✔ Advanced

Materials: poster board, crayons or markers, magazines

- Have students work together in small groups.
- Have them draw a circle in the center of a poster board and write *States of Matter* in it. Then, ask them to draw three other circles and connect them to the inner circle with lines. The three new circles should be labeled at the top with *solid*, *liquid*, and *gas*.
- Have students cut out pictures from magazines of solids, liquids, and gases.
- Have them organize the pictures and paste them onto the poster board in the appropriate sections.
- Ask the groups to share their posters with the other groups.

Informal Assessment

Beginning	Intermediate	Advanced
Have students point to a book and complete this sentence using the word *solid*, *liquid*, or *gas*. The book is a _____. *(solid)* Repeat for the examples water and air. *(Answers: liquid, gas)*	Have each student write a sentence to give an example of a solid, liquid, and gas. *(Answers will vary.)*	Have each student write at least one sentence each to define a solid, liquid, and gas. *(Solids have a specific shape and size. Liquids have a specific size, but can change shape. Gases have no specific shape or size.)*

Name _____

Date _____

Identify the State

In the first two columns, write *yes* or *no* in each box to identify the properties of solids, liquids, and gases. In the last column, write an example.

	Certain Shape?	Certain Size?	Example
Solid			
Liquid			
Gas			

School-Home Connection: Have students take this page home to share with family members. They can use this page to tell about the states of matter.

How Does Matter Change?

① Build Background

Access Prior Knowledge

When to Use	Proficiency Levels
Before introducing the lesson 15 minutes	✔ Beginning ✔ Intermediate Advanced

Give students an opportunity to discuss details they remember about mixing or putting foods together. They may need suggestions, such as tossing a salad or mixing syrup or powder into milk. Ask them to identify what they mixed together, how they combined the ingredients, and how the results came out. Did the parts mix together or stay separate?

Preteach Lesson Vocabulary

> mixture, solution

List the vocabulary words on the board.

- Have students find *mixture* on page 394. Write *mixture* on the board. Ask students what word they recognize in it. Circle *mix*.

- Ask volunteers to explain, act out, or pantomime what it means to mix two things.

- Summarize that *mix* means "to put different things together," and a *mixture* is "a combination of different things." Explain that in science a mixture combines two or more different kinds of matter. Suggest vegetable salad or fruit salad as an example of a mixture. Ask students to find classroom examples, such as pens and pencils in a jar.

- Have students find *solution* on page 395. Point out that *solution* has different meanings. An answer to a problem, for example, is called a solution. Explain that in science a solution is a special kind of mixture where the objects mix together completely, like chocolate syrup and milk. Ask students for other examples.

Build Fluency

Have students work in groups of four. Have each student write or draw a type of fruit on an index card. Have students use the names of the fruits to complete these sentences and read them together for the class.

We are making a fruit salad. Our mixture has _____, _____, _____, and _____.

© Harcourt

② Scaffold the Content

Preview the Lesson

When to Use With pp. 390–396 ⏱ 20 minutes	Proficiency Levels ✔ Beginning ✔ Intermediate ✔ Advanced

- Refer students to the picture on page 390 and read the caption. Have students discuss what they see in the picture and explain how sand and water is a mixture used to make the sand castle.
- Have students preview the section heads in the lesson and point out that they will be learning about *physical changes* and *chemical changes.*
- Summarize that physical changes, like folding paper, change the physical properties of the object without making a new substance. Chemical changes, like burning paper, make new substances.

Investigate, p. 391

Materials: measuring cup, measuring spoon, plastic spoon

- Before students begin the Investigate, help them clarify the names of the tools (*measuring cup vs. measuring spoon*, and *measuring spoon vs. plastic spoon*). Have them write the names and draw the objects on separate index cards. They can then match the names and pictures or use the cards to play a Concentration game.
- Review that *measure* means "to use tools to find the properties of an object." *Observe* means "to use the senses to learn about an object." *Record* means "to write down measurements or observations."

Modify Instruction—Multilevel Strategies

Background/Experience The concept of changes in matter, the focus of this lesson, involves understanding the differences between mixtures and solutions. These activities will help students define each term and give examples.

Beginning Ask students to name an example of a mixture and justify their choice. Repeat for a solution.

Intermediate Have students act out with props or pantomime making a mixture. Direct them to identify what they are mixing, explain what they are doing to make the mixture, and describe the results. Repeat for a solution. Encourage students to explain how the mixture and the solution are different.

Advanced Have students copy the following sentences: *Tom puts sugar in his lemonade. Sue puts milk in her cereal.* Help students read the sentences and then ask them to label each one with *mixture* or *solution.* Encourage students to write one other simple sentence to describe making a mixture and one to describe making a solution.

© Harcourt

For All Students Have students write two lists—one with examples of mixtures and one with solutions. They can expand the lists as they work through the lesson.

Extend

Have the students complete the **Show What You Know** activity on page 159 to demonstrate their understanding of mixtures and solutions.

③ Apply and Assess

Make a Picture Display

When to Use With Reading Review p. 397 20 minutes	Proficiency Levels ✔ Beginning ✔ Intermediate ✔ Advanced

Materials: paper, crayons or color pencils or markers, poster board

- Have students work together in groups of three to five to draw and label pictures of physical changes and chemical changes.
- Have groups organize all of the pictures on poster board in two columns, one titled *Physical Changes* and the other titled *Chemical Changes*.
- Ask each group to explain their drawings and what made the change occur.

Informal Assessment

Beginning	Intermediate	Advanced
Show each student a picture of a mixture and a picture of a solution. Tell them that one of the pictures shows a mixture and the other shows a solution. Have them point to each picture and tell which one is which. *(Answers should reflect the correct identification of a mixture and a solution.)*	Have each student list one way they can make a mixture and one way they can make a solution. *(Possible answer: Make a mixture by mixing lettuce, tomatoes, and cucumbers in a salad. Make a solution by dissolving sugar in hot tea.)*	Have students write one sentence to define *mixture* and one sentence to define *solution*. *(A mixture combines two or more objects. A solution is a kind of mixture in which the objects mix evenly.)*

© Harcourt

Draw and Label Mixtures and Solutions

Read the ingredients in the first column of each row. Draw a picture in the second column. Then write *mixture* or *solution* in the third column.

Ingredients	Drawing	Mixture or Solution?
Lemonade: lemon juice, water, and sugar		
Fruit Salad: grapes, banana, and apple		
Bracelet: wood and plastic beads		
Dishwater: water and liquid soap		
Chocolate Milk: milk and chocolate syrup		

School-Home Connection: Have students take this page home to share with family members. They can use this page to tell about mixtures and solutions.

12 Energy

Develop Scientific Concepts and Vocabulary

In this chapter, students will learn the physics of energy, particularly about forms of energy, how energy can be used, and the resources that produce energy. Students will also learn about saving energy.

Preview Scientific Principles

Walk through the chapter with students, pausing to read aloud or to have volunteers read aloud the three questions that are lesson titles. Encourage students to briefly discuss each question and to tell what they already know that might help them answer the questions.

When to Use With Chapter Opener	Proficiency Levels
🕐 20 minutes	✔ Beginning ✔ Intermediate ✔ Advanced

Lesson 1: What Is Energy?

- Ask students yes/no questions about what makes things move.
- Have student pairs take turns acting as robots and giving directions to move an arm or a leg or make other motions. Talk about where they think the energy comes from to make their muscles move.
- Have students find pictures of things in magazines that show energy. Ask students to cut them out and paste them onto sheets of paper, then write labels or captions for each of their photos that tell about the energy shown.
- Ask students if they think things that aren't moving have energy. Allow a few minutes of discussion. Then tell students they will learn the answer in this chapter.

Lesson 2: How Can Energy Be Used?

- Have students point to things around the room that use energy, such as lights, computers, pencil sharpeners, and their own muscles.
- Give students examples of how energy is used to change things around their homes, such as heating food, drying clothes, cooling air, and so on. Ask them to help you add things to the list.
- Show students a thermometer. Tell them this is one way to measure energy. Have students describe how to use a thermometer.

Lesson 3: Why Is Energy Important?

- Invite students to talk about how machines use energy to make them move. Point out that lots of machines need electricity to run, and cars need gasoline or electricity to run. Ask students what their bodies need to run.
- Remind students that they need food to have energy. Take a bite from a piece of fruit. Ask students how easy it is to get more fruit. If students respond, "Go to the store and buy more," ask questions to lead them to think about how the fruit is grown.
- Ask students what they can do to save energy every day. Then ask why they think it's important to save energy.

Practice

To help students understand the concept of energy, create a simple mechanical toy that demonstrates how energy moves or changes something. Have an assortment of materials available, such as small springs, string, straws, craft sticks, marbles, and elastic bands. Invite students to brainstorm how they might use these materials to move a marble from one point to another without touching it with their hands. Decide as a class what ideas would work best and then create the toy. Have students manipulate the toy one at a time. Talk about how energy was used to move the marble.

Apply

List the vocabulary words from the chart below. Read the words to students and ask if anyone knows or can guess what each one means. Have students copy the words into a notebook or on lined paper. Tell students that they will add definitions as they learn more about the words.

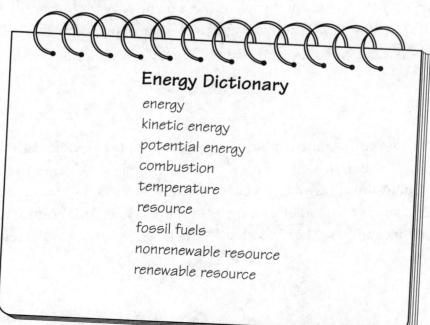

Energy Dictionary

energy
kinetic energy
potential energy
combustion
temperature
resource
fossil fuels
nonrenewable resource
renewable resource

1

What Is Energy?

① Build Background

Access Prior Knowledge

When to Use	Proficiency Levels
Before introducing the lesson	✔ Beginning
🕐 15 minutes	✔ Intermediate
	Advanced

Materials: small slips of paper, other small objects

Direct students to think about what makes things move.

• Place a few small slips of paper on a desk.

• Ask students one at a time to demonstrate ways to move the paper.

• Repeat with other small objects and ask students to compare which ones take more effort, or energy, to move.

Preteach Lesson Vocabulary

energy, kinetic energy, potential energy

Material: ball

List the vocabulary words on the board.

Remind students that they used energy to make the objects move.

• Bounce a ball and say "kinetic." Explain that anything that moves has kinetic energy.

• Bounce the ball again and have students repeat after you, "kinetic energy."

• Hold the ball up and explain that it also has potential energy. Potential energy changes into kinetic energy when there is movement. Bounce the ball again and hold it. Have students repeat after you, "potential energy."

• Bounce and hold the ball a few more times, repeating the phrases with the class.

Build Fluency

Have students stand up and form a large circle. Stand in the middle with the ball. As you bounce the ball to a student, say "kinetic energy." Say "potential energy" as the student holds the ball. Invite all the students to say "kinetic energy" and "potential energy" as the student bounces the ball back to you. Bounce the ball to other students and have the class chant "kinetic energy/potential energy" with each bounce.

© Harcourt

② Scaffold the Content

Preview the Lesson

Ask students to point to the title on page 406 as you read it aloud. Have students find the highlighted word on page 408 and follow along as you read the sentence: *Energy is the ability to make something move or change.*

- Ask students to look at the pictures on pages 408 and 409.
- Ask students to point to or describe what is moving or changing in each picture as you read aloud the captions.

Investigate, p. 407

Before the students begin the Investigate, create the groups so that beginning and intermediate students are grouped with advanced students.

- Demonstrate recording temperatures once every hour using a toy clock to advance time one hour and then pointing to the thermometer. Repeat this several times.
- Lead students to share their charts and make their inferences as a class.

Extend

Have the students complete the **Show What You Know** activity on page 165 to demonstrate their understanding of what makes temperature rise.

Modify Instruction—Multilevel Strategies

Comprehensible Input To help students understand the forms of energy and the concept of changing energy, simplify the language for them. Use the phrases "moving energy" for "kinetic energy" and "stored energy" for "potential energy."

Beginning Have students point to examples of stored energy, such as light switches and water faucets. Direct students to show you how stored energy changes to moving energy and back to stored energy.

Intermediate Have pairs of students identify forms of energy and direct each other to change stored energy to moving energy and back.

Advanced Have students describe three examples of moving energy and their sources.

For All Students Continue the lesson by reminding students that energy changes depending on position and movement.

③ Apply and Assess

Make an Energy Mobile

When to Use	Proficiency Levels
With Reading Review p. 413 ⏱ 30 minutes	✔ Beginning ✔ Intermediate ✔ Advanced

Materials: crayons, paper, string, straws, paper clips, wood dowels or sticks, scissors

Explain that students will make a mobile about energy. Have a model prepared to show as an example.

- Have students cut or tear three or four shapes of paper and draw or color designs on each one to show what they think energy looks like.
- Help students punch holes near the top of each paper shape and loop a length of string through each. Make sure enough string hangs below the straw to allow the paper shape to move freely. Tie all strings to one wood dowel or stick. Tie another length of string to each end of the dowel for hanging or holding the mobile.
- Have students hang or hold their mobiles up and see the kinetic energy of the shapes.

Informal Assessment

Beginning	Intermediate	Advanced
Ask students to use their bodies to demonstrate potential energy and kinetic energy. *(Answers will vary but should demonstrate an understanding of changes in energy.)*	Have students copy these sentence starters and complete them. A ball in my hands has _____ energy. A bouncing ball has kinetic _____. *(potential; energy)*	Ask students to write three sentences, each describing a different source of energy and how it changes or moves something. *(Answers may include: the sun, water, wind, electrical energy)*

Name _____

Date _____

Timing the Rise of Temperature

1. Draw a sun, clock, and thermometer in each box.

2. Show a different time of day on each clock.

3. Color each thermometer to show how much the temperature rose. On the back, write a sentence about what you observed.

1.	2.	3.

School-Home Connection: Have students take this page home to share with family members. They can use their pictures to tell about how temperature rises.

© Harcourt

Lesson 2: How Can Energy Be Used?

① Build Background

Access Prior Knowledge

When to Use	Proficiency Levels
Before introducing the lesson	✔ Beginning
🕐 15 minutes	✔ Intermediate
	Advanced

Have students think about how they use different sources of energy. Ask:

- How can you use the energy you get from eating food?
- How can you use the energy that comes from the sun?
- How can you use the energy that comes from a hot fire?
- How can you use the energy that comes from electricity?

Preteach Lesson Vocabulary

> **combustion, temperature**

List the vocabulary words on the board.

- Make fists with your hands and fling them open to symbolize combustion as you use the vocabulary word.
- Ask students what happens when heat energy is made. Elicit that it raises the temperature of things. Ask how we can measure temperature.

Build Fluency

Have groups of students act out the concept of combustion using body movements such as fists flinging out to open hands or hugged knees flinging out to a full body stretch.

© Harcourt

(2) Scaffold the Content

Preview the Lesson

Ask students to point to the title on page 414 as you read it aloud. Have a volunteer tell what is happening in the photo on this page. Point out that cooking is one way we use heat energy.

Ask students to follow along as you read the captions on pages 416 and 417. Talk about how the train uses energy. Invite volunteers to answer the question posed in the caption. Elicit correct use of the vocabulary word *combustion*.

Investigate, p. 415

Before the students begin Investigate, group the students in mixed-ability groups of four.

- Assign a different step of the activity to each group member as appropriate.
- Make sure students understand how to use a table to record data and how to transfer their data to a bar graph. Demonstrate as necessary.
- Use the word *guess* to help define *infer*.

Extend

Have the children complete the **Show What You Know** activity on page 169 to demonstrate their understanding of heat energy.

Modify Instruction—Multilevel Strategies

Comprehensible Input Clip magazine photos that show various forms of energy in use. Distribute to students. Write the question, *How can energy be used?* on the board.

Beginning Have students circle details in the photos that show energy being used.

Intermediate Ask students how the photo they were given answers this question. Have them discuss their answer.

Advanced Have students write their answer to the question, using several photos for reference.

For All Students Continue the lesson by reminding students to think about how energy can be measured.

© Harcourt

③ Apply and Assess

Make a Sequence Chart

When to Use	Proficiency Levels
With Reading Review p. 419  30 minutes	✔ Beginning ✔ Intermediate ✔ Advanced

Materials: crayons, copies of a blank 3-box sequence chart

- Model a completed sequence chart showing how wood produces energy that makes a fire. People use the heat from the fire to warm themselves. Tell students they will draw their own sequence charts to show other ways that energy can be used.

- Provide some ideas by writing the words *sun*, *gasoline*, and *electricity* on the board.

- Have students choose an energy source and draw it in the first box of their charts.

- In the second box, direct students to draw something that shows how the energy source changes or moves.

- In the third box, ask students to draw how a person uses the energy in the second box.

- Have volunteers explain their sequence charts to the class.

Informal Assessment

Beginning	Intermediate	Advanced
Ask students to act out one way that energy can be used. *(Answers will vary but should demonstrate understanding of a form of energy being used to move or change something.)*	Have students complete these sentence starters: Combustion happens when we _____ fuels. It produces _____. *(burn; energy)*	Ask students to write a paragraph about three ways that energy is used every day in their lives and where that energy comes from. *(Answers will vary.)*

Changes Caused by Heat

1. Draw a picture of something that produces heat energy. *(Hint: the sun or a stove.)*

2. Draw your favorite object.

3. Draw how the heat energy changes the object. On the back, write a sentence about your drawings.

1.
2.
3.

School-Home Connection: Have students take this page home to share with family members. They can use their pictures to tell about heat energy.

① Build Background

Access Prior Knowledge

When to Use	Proficiency Levels
Before introducing the lesson 🕐 15 minutes	✔ Beginning ✔ Intermediate ✔ Advanced

Ask students what they know about electricity.

- How do we use electricity?
- How do you think it is made?
- Is electricity important? What might our lives be like without it?

Preteach Lesson Vocabulary

> resource, fossil fuels, renewable resource, nonrenewable resource

Materials: photos of oil drills or rigs, coal mines, and gas pipelines

List the vocabulary words on the board.

- Show students photos of oil drills or rigs, coal mines, and gas pipelines. Explain that oil, coal, and gas are resources called *fossil fuels.*
- Show an actual fossil or a picture of one. Talk about how long it takes to make a fossil. Relate that the fossil and the oil come from things that used to live on Earth long ago.
- Circle *new* in the middle of each of the last two vocabulary words. Then underline *re-* in each word. Tell students that the prefix *re-* means "again." Elicit that *renew* means "to make new again, or to start over."
- Circle *-able* in each word. Point out that *able* means "can be." Elicit that *renewable* means "can be made new again."
- Ask students to identify the additional prefix in the second word. Remind them that *non-* means "not." Ask students what they think a *nonrenewable* resource might be. Elicit that nonrenewable resources cannot be made new again.

Build Fluency

Arrange a number of photos of both renewable and nonrenewable resources in front of the class. Make a sign for each category and attach the signs to the front edges of two desks. Tell students to sort the photos into these two categories. Hold up the photos one at a time and ask students on which desk they belong. Say "renewable" and "nonrenewable" as you place one in each category. Then have the class tell you where to put each photo.

© Harcourt

② Scaffold the Content

When to Use With pp. 420–424 15 minutes	Proficiency Levels ✔ Beginning ✔ Intermediate ✔ Advanced

Preview the Lesson

Ask students to point to the title on page 420 as you read it aloud. Ask what they see in the photo. Have them follow along as you read the caption.

Read the headings on pages 422–424. Focus on the phrase "save energy" and rephrase it for students in the context of possibly using up all the nonrenewable resources that make energy.

Investigate, p. 421

Before the students begin the Investigate, clarify the concept of a model versus a full-scale structure by making a small paper model of a chair or a desk.

- Talk about how big windmills can be and some of the ways they are used.
- Then, have students create their model windmills.

Modify Instruction—Multilevel Strategies

Comprehensible Input To reinforce the concepts of renewable and nonrenewable resources and why it is important to save energy, use the photos of resources from the Build Background section of this lesson.

Beginning Ask students to point to photos of nonrenewable and renewable resources as you cue them.

Intermediate Have student pairs use the photos as flashcards to ask and answer the questions, "Is this a renewable resource?" "Is this a nonrenewable resource?" "Why?"

Advanced Ask small groups to use the photos as props for a short presentation that identifies renewable energy sources and ways to save energy.

For All Students Continue the lesson by reminding students to think about other energy resources.

Extend

Have the students complete the **Show What You Know** activity on page 173 to demonstrate their understanding of renewable and nonrenewable resources.

③ Apply and Assess

Make an Energy Diorama

When to Use	Proficiency Levels
With Reading Review p. 425	✔ Beginning
🕐 30 minutes	✔ Intermediate
	✔ Advanced

Materials: shoe boxes, sheets of oaktag or cardboard, crayons, construction paper, paste, scissors

Have students work in mixed ability groups.

- Tell students they will create a diorama showing how people can save energy.
- Have groups plan their diorama by thinking about what energy resource they want to show and how people can save energy produced by that resource. Model that students could divide their diorama into two or more parts or use the whole space for one scene.
- Ask students to write a caption for their diorama that tells why energy is important.
- Display the dioramas and invite groups to describe their work to the class. Ask each group why they think energy is important.

Informal Assessment

Beginning	Intermediate	Advanced
Ask students to act out a way they can save energy in their lives, and to tell what they are doing. *(Answers will vary but their actions and words should agree.)*	Have students copy this sentence frame and complete it. A resource that can be replaced is _____. A resource that cannot be replaced is _____. *(renewable; nonrenewable)*	Ask students to write three sentences, each describing a different way they can save energy. *(Answers will vary.)*

ESL Support

Writing About Energy Resources

1. Draw or write examples of each kind of resource.

2. Draw or write how that resource is used to make energy.

3. Draw or write an example of how to save that energy. On the back, write a sentence about why this energy is important.

	Renewable Resources	Nonrenewable Resources
1.		
2.		
3.		

School-Home Connection: Have students take this page home to share with family members. They can use their pictures to tell about energy resources.

13 Electricity and Magnets

Develop Scientific Concepts and Vocabulary

In this chapter, students will learn about static and current electricity and about magnets. They will also discover how electricity and magnets work together in generators and electromagnets.

Preview Scientific Principles

Walk through the chapter with students, pausing to read aloud or to have volunteers read aloud the three questions that are lesson titles. Encourage students to briefly discuss each question and tell what they already know that might help them answer it.

When to Use With Chapter Opener	Proficiency Levels
🕐 20 minutes	✔ Beginning ✔ Intermediate ✔ Advanced

Lesson 1: What Is Electricity?

- Discuss with students the word *electricity*, possibly modeling how to look it up in a dictionary. Use the word in sentences to illustrate meaning, and then have volunteers generate own sentences.
- Divide the word *electricity* into syllables and have students clap for each syllable. Then ask them to pronounce each syllable with you before blending the syllables back into one word.
- Have students name ways we use electricity at school and in their homes.

Lesson 2: What Are Magnets?

- Explain that a magnet is an object that attracts iron and some other metals. A magnet can be used to make electricity.
- Encourage volunteers to share their experiences with magnets, using sentences as much as possible.

Lesson 3: How Are Electricity and Magnets Related?

- Ask students how they think electricity and magnets are related.
- Explain that magnets are used to make electricity in generators and other machinery. Some magnets can be turned off and on by electricity.

© Harcourt

Practice

Have students write each vocabulary term from this chapter on a large index card. On the back of each card, have them write, or dictate to you, questions they have about that term.

As students progress through this chapter, they can try to answer the questions on the back of the cards. They can also use the cards to create a vocabulary game.

Apply

Write the following chart on the board and have students take turns echoing or reading the sentences aloud. You might pantomime some of the actions described in the sentences and have students copy you. Then ask them to cut pictures of electrical machines and magnets out of old magazines and create a collage. Finally have each student select one picture of an electrical machine or magnet to write or tell about.

Elementary Electricity

My mom cooks on her electric stove.
The bar magnet sticks on the refrigerator door.
I have to be careful when I plug an electrical cord into the wall.
You use a switch to turn the lights on.
To save electricity, I use sunlight coming in the window.
Earth is one big magnet.
You turn on the electric air conditioner to cool off.
Thanks to electricity, I can listen to my favorite songs all day long.

Lesson 1 — What Is Electricity?

① Build Background

Access Prior Knowledge

When to Use	Proficiency Levels
Before introducing the lesson 15 minutes	✔ Beginning ✔ Intermediate Advanced

Encourage students to talk about their experiences related to electricity. Ask them to identify things in the classroom that are powered by electricity. Discuss how the classroom gets light, in addition to the light that comes through the window. How do they think classrooms were lighted long ago, before electricity was invented?

Preteach Lesson Vocabulary

> **static electricity, current electricity, circuit**

List the vocabulary words on the board.

Have students find these terms on pages 436 and 437. Invite volunteers to read the definitions that follow each term. Then:

- Ask if students ever heard or felt a crackling noise when they touched a sock or other clothing that had just came out of the dryer. Explain that this is *static electricity*. Point to the term and have students repeat it after you.
- Have students find electric cords in the room. Guide them to understand that the cords carry electricity. This kind of electricity is called *current electricity*. Have students repeat the term after you.
- Ask where the electricity that runs through the cords comes from. Explain that when the cord is plugged into the wall, current electricity flows through it. Its path is called a *circuit*. Point to the word *circuit* and have students repeat it.

Build Fluency

Have students work in pairs. One partner will ask a question such as the following, and the other partner will provide the answer in a dialogue.

- What is static electricity? It's an electric charge that builds up in an object.
- What kind of electricity moves through a cord? That is called *current electricity*.

© Harcourt

② Scaffold the Content

When to Use	Proficiency Levels
With pp. 435–438	✔ Beginning
⏱ 20 minutes	✔ Intermediate
	✔ Advanced

Preview the Lesson

- Ask students to point to the title on page 434 as you read it aloud. Explain that they will find the answer to this question in the lesson. Have students scan the lesson headings to find a possible location for the answer.
- Ask students to tell what is happening in the pictures on pages 436 to 438. What kind of electricity might a lightning flash be? *It's a charge that builds up in a cloud, so it's static electricity.*
- Discuss what kind of electricity a battery might be. Take a vote on how many students think it is static and how many think it is current. Explain that they will check their predictions later.

Investigate, p. 435

Before students begin the Investigate:

- Write the words *hypothesize* and *hypothesis* on the board. Say them and have students repeat them. Stress the long /i/ sound and the voiced ending /z/ in *hypothesize* and the short /i/ sound and voiceless ending /s/ in *hypothesis*.
- Ask what students think the words mean. Explain that a hypothesis is really a guess, but not a wild one. It is based on what you know, what you see, and what you expect to happen.
- When you hypothesize, you are making a guess, a hypothesis. *Hypothesize* is a verb, or action word, and *hypothesis* is a noun, or naming word.

Modify Instruction—Multilevel Strategies

Language and Vocabulary Have students find the word *light* on page 437. Write it on the board and have the class say it with you. Explain that *light* can be a naming word (noun), an action word (verb), or a describing word (adjective). Ask students to find *light* used as a verb and an adjective on page 437. (In *to light* and *Make It Light*, the word is a verb and in *light bulb*, it's an adjective.)

Explain that *light* has more than one meaning. For example: *Is your book light or heavy?* In this sentence, *light* means "not heavy."

Beginning Write *back* and *close* on the board. Use words and gestures to explain two meanings for each word. Then say a sentence and have students indicate the correct meaning. Examples: *I'm going back home.* (direction) *I see a bug on your back.* (body part) *Don't stand so close.* (position) *Please close the door.* (not open)

© Harcourt

Intermediate Follow the activity above, adding the word *charge* ("electrical energy, payment"). Help students use the three words in sentences or have them echo your sentences. Discuss the meanings of the words in each sentence.

Advanced Have students find other words with multiple meanings, such as *record* on page 435 and *current* on page 437. Have them write sentences using both meanings of the words.

For All Students Ask students to suggest words for a running list of terms that have more than one meaning.

Extend

Have the students complete the **Show What You Know** activity on page 179 to demonstrate their understanding of electricity.

③ Apply and Assess

Make a Picture Display

When to Use With Reading Review p. 439 ⏱ 20 minutes	Proficiency Levels ✔ Beginning ✔ Intermediate ✔ Advanced

Materials: research sources, printer or copier, scissors, construction paper

- Have groups of three or four find out how Benjamin Franklin, Thomas Edison, or other scientists helped to discover the light bulb and other electrical devices. Groups might use the Internet, with your guidance, and encyclopedias and reference books.

- Have them print out information and pictures or copy them from reference books.

- Have the groups display their pictures and share one or two interesting things they learned with the rest of the class.

Informal Assessment

Beginning	Intermediate	Advanced
Ask each student to point to pictures of examples of current and static electricity. Or point to the pictures and have students name the type of electricity. *(Answers will vary.)*	Have each student use a sentence to describe a conductor or an insulator. *(Answers will vary but may include: Electricity moves through a conductor.)*	Have each student think about the Insta-Lab on page 437 and draw a conclusion about what kind of electricity a battery provides. *(In the activity, wires touch the battery, so it must provide current electricity.)*

Name _____

Date _____

Comparing Kinds of Electricity

Use this Venn diagram to show how static and current electricity are the same and different.

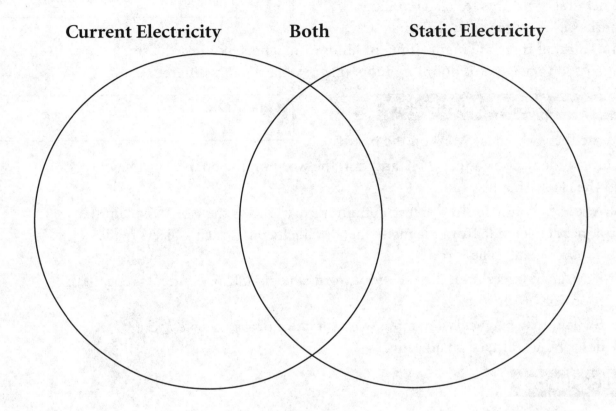

Current Electricity   **Both**   **Static Electricity**

School-Home Connection: Have students take this page home to share with family members. They can use the information to tell what they have learned about electricity.

2 What Are Magnets?

① Build Background

Access Prior Knowledge

When to Use	Proficiency Levels
Before introducing the lesson ⏱ 15 minutes	✔ Beginning ✔ Intermediate ✔ Advanced

Encourage students to talk about any experiences they have had with magnets. Point out that there are many different kinds of magnets, not just the small ones that stick on refrigerator doors, and that magnets have many different uses.

Preteach Lesson Vocabulary

> magnetic

Write the vocabulary word on the board.

Have students look at page 442 and find the word on the board. Say the word with the class. Then:

- Ask for a volunteer to read the definition that follows the word. Explain that a magnet is made from magnetic metal. This metal attracts objects made of another metal called iron.

- Have a volunteer underline the root word (*magnet*). Have students repeat the root word with you.

- Explain that *magnet* is a naming word, or a noun, and *magnetic* is a describing word, or an adjective.

Build Fluency

Have students work in pairs. One partner will ask a question such as the following, and the other partner will provide the answer in a dialogue.

- Do you know what magnets are? Yes, some of them are sticking on our refrigerator.

- What kinds of poles do magnets have? They have north and south poles.

© Harcourt

② Scaffold the Content

Preview the Lesson

When to Use	Proficiency Levels
With pp. 441–444	✔ Beginning
⏱ 20 minutes	✔ Intermediate
	✔ Advanced

- Ask students to point to the title on page 440 and explain that they will find the answer to this question in the lesson.

- Ask students to look at the pictures on pages 442 to 444 and tell what is happening. Do they think magnets can attract any object or only objects with iron in them? *(only objects with iron in them)*

- Explain that compasses have magnets in them. In which direction does the needle always point? *(north)*

- Point out that Earth has two ends, the North Pole and the South Pole. Explain that magnets also have two ends, the north pole and the south pole.

Investigate, p. 442

Before students begin the Investigate:

- Write the word *horseshoe* on the board and have students say it with you and define it. Explain that a horseshoe magnet has the shape of a horseshoe. Explain that *horseshoe* is a compound word because it is formed by putting two words together.

- Have students find the term *paper clip* on page 441. This is an open compound word because there is a space between the words. *Horseshoe* is a closed compound word because it has no space between the words.

Modify Instruction—Multilevel Strategies

Comprehensible Input Write the word *iron* on the board and have students say it with you. Explain that iron is found in many objects, such as paper clips. Magnets attract iron and steel (which is made from iron), so magnets attract things made of iron and steel, including paper clips and horseshoes.

Beginning Have students identify classroom objects that may be made of iron or steel, such as chair legs or a television stand. Have them use magnets to see whether these objects have iron in them.

Intermediate Ask students to name the two ends or poles of magnets. *(north pole, south pole)* Ask if poles that are alike attract or push each other away. Model a complete answer and have students say it with you: *Poles that are alike push each other away.*

Advanced Have students draw a magnet, label its poles, and write a paragraph describing how the poles affect each other. Have them display their work.

For All Students Encourage students to test objects at school and at home to see whether they are made of iron or steel and can attract a magnet.

Extend

Have the students complete the **Show What You Know** activity on page 183 to demonstrate their understanding of magnets and their different uses.

③ Apply and Assess

Make a Researched Presentation

Organize groups of three or four and assign each group one of these tasks:

When to Use	Proficiency Levels
With Reading Review p. 445 ⏱ 20 minutes	✔ Beginning ✔ Intermediate ✔ Advanced

- Use the Internet (with your guidance), encyclopedias, or other reference books to identify different kinds of magnets and their uses.
- Look in the dictionary to find other words based on the root *magnet*.
- Research a type of rock that the ancient Greeks and Chinese used as a magnet. *(lodestone)*
- Find out why many scientists say that Earth is one big magnet.

Have each group present its findings to the class.

Informal Assessment

Beginning	Intermediate	Advanced
Ask each student to point to pictures of horseshoe magnets, bar magnets, and paper clips as you name them. Or you might point to the pictures and ask students to name them. *(Answers will vary.)*	Have each student describe magnets in a sentence. *(Answers will vary. Example: Magnets attract objects made of iron.)*	Have each student describe how poles affect each other in magnets. *(Answers will vary. Example: Like poles push each other away, while opposite poles attract each other.)*

© Harcourt

Name _____

Date _____

Webbing Magnets

Complete this word web with four words from the box below.

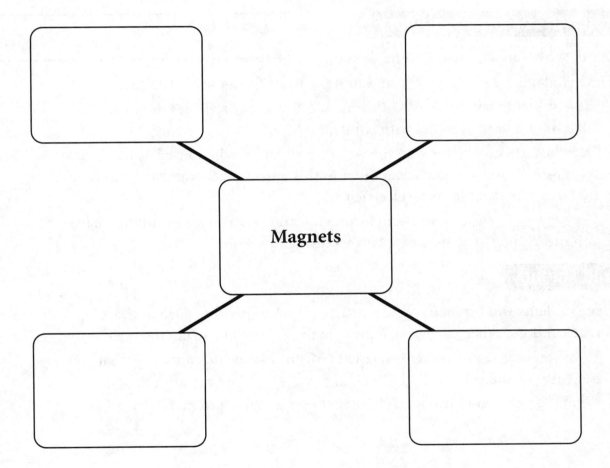

plastic	steel	nails
rubber	paper	horseshoe

Magnets

© Harcourt

School-Home Connection: Have students take this page home so they can share what they are learning about magnets with family members.

Lesson 3

How Are Electricity and Magnets Related?

① Build Background

Access Prior Knowledge

When to Use	Proficiency Levels
Before introducing the lesson 15 minutes	✔ Beginning ✔ Intermediate ✔ Advanced

Invite students to talk about their experiences related to magnets and electricity. Discuss what people in public buildings, such as schools and hospitals, do when they have no electricity due to a storm or other emergency.

Preteach Lesson Vocabulary

generator

Write the vocabulary word on the board.

Have students look at page 450 and find the word from the board. Then:

- Have students say the word with you. Ask how many syllables the word has. Clap out the four syllables with students.
- Demonstrate how to look up the word *generator* in a dictionary. Have volunteers read the meanings. Explain that in this lesson, a generator is a machine that uses a magnet to make electricity.
- Use the word *generator* in a sentence to illustrate its meaning, and then have volunteers offer sentences of their own using this word.

Build Fluency

Have students work in pairs. One partner will ask a question such as the following, and the other partner will provide the answer in a dialogue.

- Have you ever seen an electromagnet? No, but I know it is a magnet that you can turn on and off.
- What is a generator? It is a machine that uses a magnet to make electricity.

© Harcourt

② Scaffold the Content

Preview the Lesson

- Ask students to point to the title on page 446 as you read it aloud. Explain that they will find the answer to this question in the lesson. Ask if students have ever seen an electromagnet lift a car. How did that happen?
- Have students look at the pictures on pages 448 to 450 and tell what is happening. Remind them that in the previous lessons they learned about electricity and magnets. Now they will find out how they are related.
- Write the word *electromagnet* on the board and have students say it with you. Explain that an electromagnet is a magnet that can be turned on and off. Large electromagnets can lift heavy metal objects, such as cars.

Investigate, p. 447

Before students begin the Investigate:

- Have them find the word *infer* and the heading *Draw Conclusions* on page 447 and repeat them after you.
- Explain that *infer* and *draw conclusions* both mean to figure something out using what you know and what you have observed.
- Have students practice inferring and drawing conclusions. For example, ask: If you see someone smiling, what can you infer? (*That person is happy about something.*) If a plate of cookies is empty, and your sister has crumbs on her shirt, what conclusion can you draw? (*She ate the cookies.*)

Modify Instruction—Multilevel Strategies

Background and Experience Help students review what they have learned about magnets and electricity by asking questions such as these: What are two kinds of electricity? (*static and current*) Which objects in the classroom are powered by electricity? (*Answers will vary.*) Why do magnets stick to some objects? (*They stick to things made of iron or steel.*) Which objects in the classroom would magnets stick to? (*Answers will vary.*)

Beginning Have students watch as you make an electromagnet from a nail or screw, wire, and a battery. Explain each step as you perform it and have students say the step after you.

Intermediate As you make an electromagnet, encourage students to copy your actions and repeat your words. Ask them to name the materials you are using.

Advanced As students watch you make an electromagnet, have them say and write the steps that you are carrying out. Then have one student tell another how to make a battery.

For All Students Have students work in small groups to draw a chart showing the steps in making an electromagnet.

Extend

Have the students complete the Show What You Know activity on page 187 to demonstrate their understanding of magnets and electricity.

③ Apply and Assess

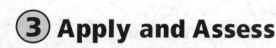

Make an Action Mural

When to Use With Reading Review p. 451 🕐 20 minutes	Proficiency Levels ✔ Beginning ✔ Intermediate ✔ Advanced

Materials: crayons, mural paper

- Have students expand on their chart of the steps in making an electromagnet by creating a mural showing one student carrying out the steps. They will draw the student performing each step and add a speech balloon in which the student describes what he or she is doing. If necessary, draw a student and show how to add a speech balloon over his or her head.

- Provide support by writing sentence frames on the board. Examples: I wrap the _____ around the nail. I connect one end of the wire to a _____.

- When the mural is finished, have volunteers read the speech balloons aloud.

Informal Assessment

Beginning	Intermediate	Advanced
Ask each student to point to pictures of magnets, electromagnets, and generators. Have them read or say these words with you. Or point to the pictures and ask students to identify them.	Have each student write a sentence describing a generator or an electromagnet. *(Answers will vary. Example: A generator uses a magnet to make electricity.)*	Have each student use sentences to tell how an electromagnet and a regular magnet are similar and different. *(Answers will vary. Example: They both attract metal objects, but an electromagnet's power can be turned on and off.)*

Name _____

Date _____

Magnets and Electricity

Read each word and draw a picture of it.

Magnets and Electricity

bar magnet

horseshoe magnet

electromagnet

generator

School-Home Connection: Have students take this page home to share with family members what they have learned about the relationship between magnets and electricity.

© Harcourt

14 Heat, Light, and Sound

Develop Scientific Concepts and Vocabulary

In this chapter, students will learn about three types of energy: *heat*, *light*, and *sound*. They will learn how heat is measured and how it moves. Students will also discover how light moves, and ways light behaves. In addition, students will connect sound with vibrations and the strength of their movement.

Preview Scientific Principles

Walk through the chapter with students, pausing to read aloud or to have volunteers read aloud the three questions that are lesson titles. Encourage students to briefly discuss each question to tell what they already know that might help them answer the questions.

When to Use With Chapter Opener	Proficiency Levels
🕐 20 minutes	✔ Beginning ✔ Intermediate ✔ Advanced

Lesson 1: What Is Heat?

- Show students a picture of a fire. Ask if anyone has been near a working fireplace or by a campfire. Have students share their experiences. Invite them to use descriptive words to tell what it felt like.

- Ask students to tell other times and places where they have felt warmth or heat.

Lesson 2: What Is Light?

- Ask students to point to the light in the classroom. Turn the light off and say "The lights are off." Then, turn it back on and say "The lights are on."

- Explain that light is a form of energy. Ask them what other things give off light.

- Turn off the classroom lights and pull the shades. Have students imagine what it would be like to see without any light at all. Discuss why light is important.

Lesson 3: How Are Light and Color Related?

- Ask students to tell what color they think light is. Then show them a picture of a rainbow. Ask them to tell how they think a rainbow is made.

- Place a clear glass jar, a jar or vase that is translucent, and an opaque plastic cup on a table. Have students try to look through each and share their observations.

© Harcourt

Lesson 4: What Is Sound?

- Ask students to be very still, with their eyes closed for a few minutes, as they listen for different sounds. Call on volunteers to imitate one sound he or she heard and to point to or to tell what they think made the sound.

Practice

To help students understand that *heat*, *light*, and *sound* are all connected, make a concept web with the word *ENERGY* in the center. Draw a branch for each of the three types of energy discussed in this chapter. Encourage students to dictate or write related words around each of the lesson focus words. For example, words related to heat might include *hot*, *warm*, *fire*, *stove*, and *cook*. Words related to light might include *bright*, *sun*, *warm*, *shine*, and so on. Sound words might include *hear*, *ears*, *noise*, *bang*, *pop*, *splash*, *crash*, and so on. Students may then use these words to write sentences related to energy.

Apply

Write the sentences from the following chart on the board and have students take turns echoing or reading each line aloud. Guide students to see how each sentence relates to a type of energy. Allow students to search old magazines for pictures that represent each type of energy. Have them cut and paste the pictures on a sheet of paper to make a collage poster. Finally, have each student select one picture to write about or to tell about.

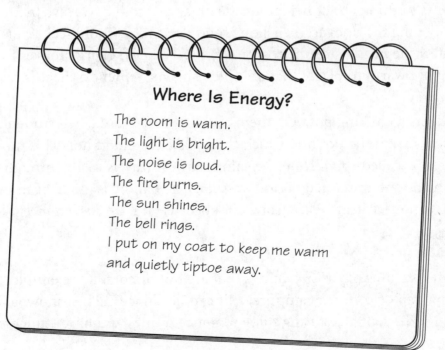

Where Is Energy?

The room is warm.
The light is bright.
The noise is loud.
The fire burns.
The sun shines.
The bell rings.
I put on my coat to keep me warm
and quietly tiptoe away.

Lesson 1 — What Is Heat?

① Build Background

Access Prior Knowledge

When to Use	Proficiency Levels
Before introducing the lesson 20 minutes	✔ Beginning ✔ Intermediate ✔ Advanced

Materials: thermometer

Pass the thermometer around and give students an opportunity to name the device. If they are not familiar with the term, say *thermometer*, and have them echo it. Then, ask if students know what a thermometer does. Write the words *hot* and *cold* on the board. Ask students to think of a time when they felt hot. Have them relate their experiences. Follow the same procedure for the word *cold*.

Preteach Lesson Vocabulary

> **temperature, heat, thermal energy, conduction, conductor, insulator**

List the vocabulary words on the board.

Have students look through the lesson to find the vocabulary words.

- Have students say *temperature*. Remind students of the thermometers they viewed before the lesson. Point out that a thermometer measures temperature.

- Ask students to think about being outside on a very cold day. Have them imagine opening the door to their house and what they would feel. Explain that they feel the *heat* inside their warm home. The *heat* energy moves from places that are warm to places that are cold. This movement of heat is called *thermal energy*.

- Show students a cooking pot. Ask them to tell how it is used. Tell students that the *heat* makes the pot hot, which then makes the food hot. This movement of heat is called *conduction*. Explain that heat travels easily through the metal in the pot because metal is a *conductor*. The handle is made of material that doesn't transfer heat well. It stays cool because it is an *insulator*.

Build Fluency

Show students pictures of various things that are hot or cold. For example, show a steaming cup of coffee, a campfire, a lit candle, an ice cube, a snowball, and ice cream. Model sentences using these sentence frames and have students repeat them.

The _____ is hot.

The _____ is cold.

© Harcourt

190 ESL Support

② Scaffold the Content

When to Use	Proficiency Levels
With pp. 460–464	✔ Beginning
	✔ Intermediate
⏱ 20 minutes	✔ Advanced

Preview the Lesson

- Direct students to the picture of the campfire on page 462. Ask if they have been near a fire like this one. Have students tell how it felt.

- Point out the frying pan on page 463. Invite students to name other things they know that are made of metal. Talk about how those items would be good heat conductors.

- Identify the materials in the items shown on page 464 and explain that they are acting as insulators. Ask students if they can think of a time when they used an insulator, such as a blanket, to stay warm as they slept. Give students an opportunity to share their experiences.

Investigate, p. 461

Before students begin the Investigate:

- Model the steps of the experiment as students follow along with their own materials. Talk through each step; explain that here *seal* means "to close tightly."

- Add drops of liquid with the dropper until the water level is above the clay.

- Show students on a clock the amount of time they are to leave their "thermometer" before checking the water level.

- Connect warmer temperatures to rising water-level readings and cooler temperatures to lower water-level readings.

Modify Instruction—Multilevel Strategies

Language and Vocabulary Draw a line dividing each word between its root and the suffix *-or* in the words *conductor* and *insulator*. Tell students that the *-or* suffix can change an action word into a noun. This suffix means "someone or something that." In science, *to conduct* means "to act as a channel or a path." Students can then define *conductor* as "something that acts as a channel or path." Explain that metal is a good conductor of heat. Then, define *insulate* as "to protect or block." Have students use what they have learned about the *-or* suffix to define *insulator* in relation to heat *(something that blocks or protects from heat)*.

Beginning Show students pictures of various items that are either conductors (metal spoon, copper pot) or insulators (wooden door, cloth oven mitt). Name each item and ask students to sort the items into two piles—conductors and insulators. Then point to the conductors and say *conductor*. Have students repeat. Do the same for the insulators.

Intermediate Use the same pictures as above. Have students sort the pictured objects by category. Then have them name the items and tell if the items are conductors or insulators by using these sentence frames: *The _____ is a conductor. The _____ is an insulator.*

Advanced Have students sort the pictured items by category. Have them name each item, identify each as a conductor or an insulator, and then tell why this is so. Students may use a sentence frame such as: *The _____ is a _____ because _____.*

For All Students Reinforce the fact that conduction is one of the ways that heat travels and is an example of thermal energy.

Extend

Have students complete the Show What You Know activity on page 193 to demonstrate their understanding of how a thermometer measures temperature.

③ Apply and Assess

Make Dictionary Pages

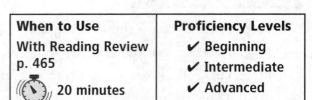

When to Use With Reading Review p. 465 ⏱ 20 minutes	Proficiency Levels ✔ Beginning ✔ Intermediate ✔ Advanced

Materials: paper and markers

- Remind students that in a dictionary, the words appear in alphabetical order.
- On the first page, have students write *conductor*. Then, using information learned from the lesson, have students write its definition. Under the definition, invite students to write or draw examples of conductors of heat.
- Have students follow the same procedure for *insulator*.
- Encourage students to read and compare their definitions and examples with a partner. Invite students to keep their pages in a three-ring binder and to add other science words throughout the year.

Informal Assessment

Beginning	Intermediate	Advanced
Show students pictures of insulators and conductors of heat. Say *conductor* and have them identify at least one conductor of heat. Do the same for insulators. *(Students should correctly identify a conductor and an insulator.)*	Ask students which of the following would be a conductor of heat: *a soft blanket, a plastic spoon, a metal fork*. Then, ask which of these would be a good insulator: *a plastic bag, a copper pot, a metal lid*. *(Metal fork; plastic bag)*	Have students explain why you might put on extra blankets during a cold night. *(Answers may vary, but students should indicate that the blankets would act as an insulator and keep heat from your body near your body.)*

© Harcourt

Name _____

Date _____

Show the Temperature

Think about the thermometer you made. For picture 1, draw what your thermometer looks like in a sunny window. For picture 2, draw what your thermometer looks like in a refrigerator. On the back, write a sentence about picture 1 or picture 2.

Picture 1	Picture 2

School-Home Connection: Have students take this page home to share with family members. Have them use their pictures to tell more about what they did on this page.

© Harcourt

Lesson **2** What Is Light?

① Build Background

Access Prior Knowledge

When to Use	Proficiency Levels
Before introducing the lesson 20 minutes	✔ Beginning ✔ Intermediate ✔ Advanced

Materials: flashlight, a clear glass, a mirror, a piece of cloth

Encourage students to shine the flashlight on each of the items and talk about what light does when the flashlight is shone on each object. Then, invite students to shine the light on other objects in the classroom and make additional observations.

Preteach Lesson Vocabulary

> reflection, refraction, shadow

Materials: mirror, glass of water, pencil, overhead projector

List the vocabulary words on the board.

- Pass around a small mirror and allow each student to look at their *reflection*. Explain that light rays bounce off your face, hit the mirror, and bounce back to your eyes.
- Place a pencil in a glass of water. Have students notice that the pencil looks bent. Tell them they are seeing a *refraction*. The pencil does not bend, but the light rays do when they enter the water.
- Use an overhead projector to cast a shadow on the wall. Tell students that the *shadow* comes from the light being blocked. Invite students to make their own shadows.

Build Fluency

Give each pair of students a small mirror. Have them take turns holding the mirror in front of objects and completing the following sentence frame to describe what they see reflected:

I see _____.

© Harcourt

② Scaffold the Content

Preview the Lesson

When to Use	Proficiency Levels
With pp. 466–470	✔ Beginning
🕐 15 minutes	✔ Intermediate
	✔ Advanced

Materials: mirror

- Tell students that they will learn more about light in this lesson.
- Point out that in the pictures on page 468, light is reflected in a straight line. Have students examine a mirror by running their hand over it. Say *smooth* and *shiny* as they observe it.
- Have students look closely at the image on page 469. Tell students that light bends as it enters water. Draw a diagram on the board to represent the path of light as it moves through the water.
- Invite students to point out the shadows that they see on page 470.

Investigate, p. 467

Before students begin the Investigate:

- Model each step of the process for students, paying special attention to the prepositions and prepositional phrases used to describe place.
- Highlight the words *on*, *in the direction of*, *between*, and *across* as you demonstrate each action.
- Help students to understand the meaning of the scientific process skills *observe*, *infer*, and *record*.

Modify Instruction—Multilevel Strategies

Background and Experience Help students to deepen their understanding of light and shadow by discussing experiences with shadows. If possible, take students outside at various times on a sunny day. Have them try to see their shadows and notice ways that shadows look different at different times of day. Use the following exercises to give students an opportunity to connect experiences of shadows with light.

Beginning Give students a flashlight, a piece of paper, and a small toy. Place the toy on top of the paper. Hold the flashlight above and slightly to the side of the toy to make a shadow on the paper. Point to and say *shadow*. Have students repeat. Then, give students an opportunity to make shadows of their own.

Intermediate Using the same materials, have students identify the shadow. Then give them the flashlight to make shadows of their own. Invite students to point out the ways that shadows look different when the light is moved into different positions. Have students use the words *shorter* and *longer* to describe the differences in shadow lengths.

Advanced Have students use the materials to make shadows of different lengths. Tell them to describe the shadows in complete sentences. Then, challenge them to find a way to shine the flashlight so that no shadow is made.

For All Students Continue to make connections between light and shadow.

Extend

Have the students complete the **Show What You Know** activity on page 197 to demonstrate their understanding of how shadows are formed.

③ Apply and Assess

Make and Draw a Shadow

When to Use With Reading Review p. 471 20 minutes	Proficiency Levels ✔ Beginning ✔ Intermediate ✔ Advanced

Materials: butcher paper, flashlights, pencils, small toys, miscellaneous school tools

- Give each pair a flashlight. Invite students to select various small toy items. Have them use the flashlight to make shadows with the objects. As one student makes a shadow, have the partner trace its outline on the paper.
- Encourage students to hold the flashlight at different angles and observe differences in the shadows that are formed.
- Pairs may discuss how the position of the light changes the length of the shadows.

Informal Assessment

Beginning	Intermediate	Advanced
Give students a flashlight to make a shadow. Point to the shadow and have students echo as you name it. Ask students to make a shadow that is long. Do the same for a shadow that is short. *(Answer: Students should be able to make shadows of different lengths.)*	Have students use a flashlight to make a shadow. Then, ask them to show ways the shadow can change. Have them use the words *short* and *long* to correctly describe the shadows that form. *(Answer: Students should be able to accurately create a long and short shadow. They should also correctly name each.)*	Give students a flashlight. Have them make long shadows and short shadows and explain why the shadow lengths change. Finally, ask them to show where to place the flashlight so that no shadow is cast. *(Answer: Students should make long shadows and short shadows and explain that reposition- ing the light source causes the length of the shadow to change. They should show a flashlight held directly above an object casting no shadow.)*

Name _____

Date _____

Shadow Lengths

Draw a picture of how you can make a long shadow with a flashlight. Draw a picture of how you can make a short shadow with a flashlight. On the back, write a sentence telling where you could put a flashlight to make no shadow.

Long Shadow

Short Shadow

School-Home Connection: Have children take this page home to share with family members. They can use this page to tell about how shadows are cast.

© Harcourt

Lesson 3 How Are Light and Color Related?

① Build Background

Access Prior Knowledge

When to Use	Proficiency Levels
Before introducing the lesson	✔ Beginning
⏱ 20 minutes	✔ Intermediate
	Advanced

Materials: photograph of a rainbow

- Display a picture of a rainbow. Say *rainbow* as students repeat.

- Ask if students know when we see a rainbow. Guide them to see that a rainbow comes just after it has rained, when the sun comes out. Invite students to make guesses about what causes a rainbow.

Preteach Lesson Vocabulary

> absorbed, opaque, transparent, translucent

Materials: sponge, shallow pan, water

List the vocabulary words on the board.

- Place a sponge in a shallow pan of water and invite students to observe what happens. Tell them that the sponge has *absorbed*, or taken in, the water.

- Explain that light is also *absorbed*, or taken in, by the things that it strikes. Point out that some objects *absorb* more light than others.

- Point to your clothing, a desk, a book, and other objects in the classroom. Tell students these objects are *opaque* and absorb most of the light that strikes them.

- Have students notice that the words *transparent* and *translucent* both begin with *trans-*, which means "across" or "through." Explain that in both words, light passes *through* something. Point out that clear glass, water, and some plastics are *transparent*, meaning that light passes through them. Glass that is not clear, such as frosted glass, still lets some light pass through, so it is called *translucent*.

Build Fluency

Help students to correctly pronounce each vocabulary word. Say each word. Next, say the words again as you clap the syllables. Invite students to repeat the words as they clap along. Then, have students work with a partner to state and echo each word.

© Harcourt

② Scaffold the Content

When to Use	Proficiency Levels
With pp. 472–478	✔ Beginning
15 minutes	✔ Intermediate
	✔ Advanced

Preview the Lesson

Materials: clear marbles, frosted marbles

- Have students find the lesson title. Read it as they follow along. Point out that the word *related* means "connected to in some way," or having some things in common.
- Ask students if they have ever seen marbles like the ones on pages 474 and 475. Pass the marbles around for students to observe by holding them up to light.
- As students look at the refracted light on page 476, have them point to the different colors they see and can identify.
- Have students follow the beams of light on page 478 to find where they all meet.

Investigate, p. 473

Before students begin the Investigate:

- Write the following words, each on a separate index card: *red*, *orange*, *yellow*, *green*, *blue*, and *violet*. Use the corresponding color crayon to color each card.
- Invite students to identify the colors in a language other than English. Then, point to the English word and say it as students repeat.
- Have students work with a partner to practice identifying each color and reading its name.
- Use the color cards to assist students as they work through the Investigate activity.

Modify Instruction—Multilevel Strategies

Background and Experience

Materials: prism, flashlight

- Remind students of how light behaves in water (the light rays bend, or refract).
- Show students a prism and name it. Shine a flashlight through the prism. Point out to students that refracted light causes the rainbow to appear. Point to it as you say *rainbow*. Tell students that, as in water, the light rays bend. The result is the breaking apart of white light into its many colors.

Use the following activities to reinforce how a prism bends light to form a rainbow.

Beginning Show students a picture of a rainbow. Point to it and say *rainbow*. Then, have students shine a flashlight through a prism. Say *prism*. Point to the colors that come through the prism and compare them to the colors of the rainbow.

Intermediate Have students use the prism and flashlight to make a rainbow. Ask them yes or no questions related to the activity. *Does the light look different as it passes through the prism? Does the light stay in a straight line as it passes through the prism?*

Advanced Have students use the prism and flashlight to make a rainbow. Then, invite them to tell why the light looks different as it passes through the prism. Have students name the colors they can see, and then name the colors in a rainbow.

For All Students Help students to see that white light is made up of all the colors. Only when white light is broken into its parts by the prism are the colors visible to the eye.

Extend

Have students complete the Show What You Know activity on page 201 to demonstrate their understanding of how a rainbow forms.

③ Apply and Assess

Making Rainbows

When to Use	Proficiency Levels
With Reading Review p. 479 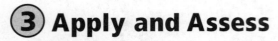 20 minutes	✔ Beginning ✔ Intermediate ✔ Advanced

Materials: clear glass, water, prism

- Give partners a clear glass filled with water. Have them hold the glass up to the sunlight and move it around in the sunlight until they see a rainbow form on its surface.

- Have students let sunlight pass through a prism. Have partners notice how this rainbow is different from the one formed by the sunlight passing through the glass of water.

Informal Assessment

Beginning	Intermediate	Advanced
Have students draw a rainbow. Then have them repeat the word *rainbow* after you. Give students a prism and a flashlight to form a rainbow. *(Answer: Students should be able to accurately draw a rainbow and use the prism and flashlight to form a rainbow.)*	Have students complete the following sentence frame: *You need _____ and _____ to see a rainbow form outside.* *(Answers: rain; sunlight)*	Have students show how to form a rainbow using a flashlight and a prism. Ask students to explain the process. Finally, have students complete the following sentence frames: *Light _____ as it passes through a prism. This separates the light into _____.* *(Answer: Students should be able to accurately describe using a prism to break apart light. Then they should complete the sentence frames with bends and different colors.)*

© Harcourt

Name _____

Date _____

The Colors of the Rainbow

Color the rainbow and label its colors. On the back, write a sentence telling
how a rainbow forms.

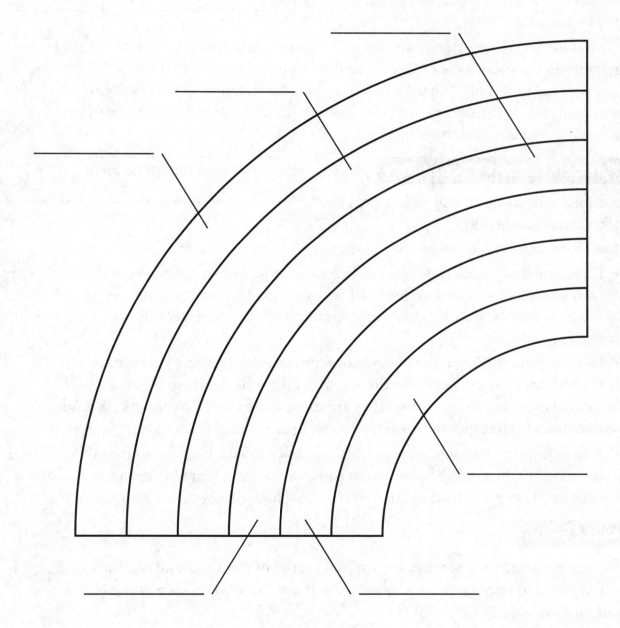

 School-Home Connection: Have children take this page home to share with
family members. They can use this page to tell about rainbows and how they form.

ESL Support   201

© Harcourt

① Build Background

Access Prior Knowledge

When to Use	Proficiency Levels
Before introducing the lesson 20 minutes	✔ Beginning ✔ Intermediate Advanced

Materials: a variety of percussion and/or string instruments

Give students an opportunity to play each of the instruments. As they do, comment on the sounds they make by saying "That was loud." "That was soft." "That was a high sound." "That was a low sound." Invite students to relate how the instruments *feel* as they play them. Draw attention to the feelings of vibration generated as the instruments are played.

Preteach Lesson Vocabulary

> **vibrations, loudness, pitch**

Materials: tambourine or drum, age-appropriate music, CD or cassette player

List the vocabulary words on the board.

- Have students put their fingers on their throat and hum a low note along with you. Ask them to describe what they feel. Explain that they are feeling the *vibration*, or movement, of their vocal cords. The movement of the cords makes sound.

- Demonstrate shaking a tambourine or tapping a drum. Then, shake or tap louder. Have students tell how the sound is different. Tell them that the sound becomes louder because they are using more energy to hit or shake the instrument. The amount of energy a sound has is called *loudness*.

- Play a portion of an age-appropriate song. Ask students if all the sounds in the song are the same. Point out that some of the sounds are higher, and some are lower. Tell students that *pitch* is how high or how low a sound is.

Build Fluency

Using a keyboard or other instrument, play a series of low notes and high notes. Invite students to respond to each sound with one of the following sentences:

That is a low sound.

That is a high sound.

© Harcourt

② Scaffold the Content

Preview the Lesson

When to Use With pp. 480–484	Proficiency Levels
⏱ 15 minutes	✔ Beginning ✔ Intermediate ✔ Advanced

- Ask students to point to the title of the lesson. Tell students that they will find the answer to this question in this lesson.

- Have students look at the picture of the harp on page 482. Guide students to see that a harp has strings that are similar to a guitar or other stringed instrument. Point to the thicker strings and say *low sounds*. Point to the thinner strings and say *high sounds*.

- Direct students to the images on page 483. Ask if students have ever swum underwater. Have them share what sounds they heard.

- Have students point to the image showing the inner ear. Say *ear* as they indicate it.

Investigate, p. 481

Before students begin the Investigate:

- Help students understand the actions in the activity before they make their maracas. Write the following words and phrases on the board: *flatten, fold it over, put tape over, staple,* and *shake*. Demonstrate each action for students.

- Help students understand that the word *compare* means to show how two things are the same and different.

Modify Instruction—Multilevel Strategies

Comprehensible Input Assist students in understanding the concept of *pitch* by having them make a string instrument of their own. Have students wear safety goggles whenever they work with rubber bands. Place two rubber bands, one thick and one thin, over an empty plastic food storage container (rectangular or square). Point to the thin "string" as you say *thin*. Pluck that rubber band as you say *high pitch*. Then point to the other band and say *thick*. Pluck it as you say *low pitch*. Give students an opportunity to explore different sounds in the following activities.

Beginning Have students pluck the rubber bands. Say *high pitch* as they pluck the thin string. Invite them to repeat. Do the same for the thick band, saying *low pitch*. Have students repeat.

Intermediate Ask students to point to the rubber band that will have a *low pitch*. Then have them pluck the string to verify their answer. Ask them what is different about this rubber band that causes it to have a lower sound than the other rubber band.

© Harcourt

Advanced Have students pluck both bands of the instrument and identify the pitch of each. Model how to press down on one end of the band and pluck the other end. Ask them to try this while moving their pressed finger up and down the band, making different sounds. Invite them to share how the sound changes.

For All Students Review with students that our ears can hear changes in pitch, as well as changes in the loudness of sound.

Extend

Have students complete the **Show What You Know** activity on page 205 to demonstrate their understanding of pitch.

③ Apply and Assess

A Classroom Band

When to Use	Proficiency Levels
With Reading Review p. 485	✔ Beginning
⏱ 20 minutes	✔ Intermediate
	✔ Advanced

Materials: miscellaneous items in the classroom

- Have students explore the classroom to find items that have different pitches when they are shaken, tapped, or manipulated in some way. Invite each student to choose one item to use as an instrument.

- Have students experiment playing their instruments at the same time. Then, have them group themselves by the pitch of the instruments. Have students whose instruments make high sounds sit in one area, while students whose instruments make low sounds sit in another area.

- Work with students to play a familiar song.

Informal Assessment

Beginning	Intermediate	Advanced
Have students look at the picture on page 482. Invite them to point to the strings that will have a low pitch. Say *low pitch*, and have them repeat. Then have them point to the strings that will have a high pitch, and say this term as students echo. *(Answer: Students should point to the long, thick strings as they say* low pitch. *They should point to the short, thin strings as they say* high pitch.*)*	After looking at page 482, have students complete the following sentence frames: *The long, thick strings have a _____ pitch. The short, thin strings have a _____ pitch. (Answer: low; high)*	Have students think about how they changed the sound on one band of their instrument. Invite them to copy and complete the following sentence frames. *I can press on the band to make _____ sounds. I make the sound higher by making the part of the band I plucked _____. I make the sound lower by making the part of the band I plucked _____. (Answer: higher and lower; shorter, longer)*

© Harcourt

Name _____

Date _____

My Instrument

Draw a picture of the instrument you made. Show the difference between the two rubber bands. Label one rubber band *low pitch* and the other rubber band *high pitch*.

School-Home Connection: Have children take this page home to share with family members. They can use this page to tell about high pitch and low pitch.

© Harcourt

15 Forces and Motion

Develop Scientific Concepts and Vocabulary

In this chapter, students will learn about forces and motion. They will gain an understanding of how speed and motion are related and how time and distance impact speed. Students will learn about kinds of force and what forces do and will also investigate different types of waves and how they move.

Preview Scientific Principles

Walk through the chapter with students, pausing to read aloud or to have volunteers read aloud the three questions that are lesson titles. Encourage students to briefly discuss each question and to tell what they already know that might help them answer the questions.

When to Use With Chapter Opener	Proficiency Levels
20 minutes	✔ Beginning ✔ Intermediate ✔ Advanced

Lesson 1: What is Motion?

- Ask students to place a pencil on their desk and observe it. Help students verbalize that the pencil does not move.

- Ask students to blow on the pencil and tell what happens.

- Invite students to move the pencil around their desk in other ways such as pushing it with their finger, tipping their desk, and so on. Have students comment on how fast or slowly the pencil moved each time.

Lesson 2: What Are Forces?

- Explain that *force* is any kind of a push or a pull. Have students sit in a circle on the floor. Give them a variety of types of objects including a book, a shoe, a basket, a stuffed animal, and a toy car. Invite students to manipulate the items and tell what kind of force they are using to move them. Have students comment on the different way that each item moves and speculate on the reasons why.

© Harcourt

Lesson 3: How Do Waves Move?

- Line chairs in a row. Have students each sit in their chair and complete a wave motion, as is often done at sporting events, by having them stand and sit in a successive order.
- Practice this movement several times until students are proficient. Then invite them to help you draw the path of motion that they followed as they moved (a wave).

Practice

To help students feel comfortable with lesson vocabulary, assist them in creating action word journals. Brainstorm action words that describe or relate to kinds of motion and forces. List the words on the board, and invite students to copy the word lists into a journal. Encourage students to add new related words to their journals as they read the lessons.

Apply

Read the story below as students follow along. Then have students copy the sentences into their action word journal. Invite them to underline all the action words. Encourage them to choose at least two of the underlined words and use them to write new sentences.

Miguel on the Move

Miguel kicked the ball.
The ball flew over the fence.
Miguel pushed the trash can over.
He climbed up to see the ball.
His neighbor grabbed the ball from the garden.
She tossed it back to Miguel.
Then Miguel passed the ball to Renee.
She hit the ball with a bat.
The ball sailed up into the air.
It bounced over the fence again.

Lesson 1 What Is Motion?

① Build Background

Access Prior Knowledge

When to Use	Proficiency Levels
Before introducing the lesson 🕐 15 minutes	✔ Beginning ✔ Intermediate Advanced

Materials: ball

Have students sit in a circle. Hold a ball on the floor in front of you. Help students verbalize that the ball is on the floor. Roll the ball to someone. Ask a volunteer to tell what happened to the ball (it moved). Have the ball rolled back to you. Say: "The ball was in one position. When I rolled the ball, it began to move. The ball changed position." Give students an opportunity to move the ball around the circle in different ways.

Preteach Lesson Vocabulary

> **motion, distance, speed**

List the vocabulary words on the board.

Have students look through the lesson to find the vocabulary words.

- Ask a volunteer to walk to the classroom door. Explain that the student is moving from one place to another. This movement, or change in position, is called *motion*.
- Have the student walk to the door once more. This time, have students count the number of steps that are taken. Explain that we use *distance* to tell how far something moves. In this example, the distance was the number of steps taken to reach the door.
- Repeat the activity again. This time, use the classroom clock to time how long it takes for the volunteer to reach the door. Tell students: "_____ walked _____ steps in _____ seconds." Explain that *speed* tells how far an object or person moves in a certain amount of time.

Build Fluency

Materials: ball

Give partners a ball. Have them move the ball in different ways and describe the motion to each other. Students may use the following sentence frame:

The ball _____.

© Harcourt

② Scaffold the Content

| When to Use
With pp. 496–502
🕐 30 minutes | Proficiency Levels
✔ Beginning
✔ Intermediate
✔ Advanced |

Preview the Lesson

- Explain that as students read the lesson, they will find the answer to the title question.

- For the images on pages 498 and 499, have students use their finger to follow each motion as you read the labels. Point out that, in the last image, the arrows indicated not only the direction, but also the speed.

- On page 500, have students read the title of the bar graph and the names of the dogs being compared. Ask questions to help students use and understand the bar graph.

- Guide students through the remaining pictures of the lesson, asking students to tell whether each picture shows something that is slow moving or fast moving.

Investigate, p. 497

Before students begin the Investigate:

- Preview the steps of the Investigate with students for words that may be unfamiliar.

- Point out that the word *mold* in step 1 means "to shape." Demonstrate how to make a ball and a ring with the clay.

- Model for students the different motions they will be moving the clay in, such as *straight* and *zigzag*.

- Call attention to the picture of the ring of clay. Show how to attach the string to the clay. Then model how to swing the ring both *back and forth* and *round and round*.

Modify Instruction—Multilevel Strategies

Language and Vocabulary This lesson involves the use of direction words that describe the path of motion. As you read the lesson with students, keep a record of the direction words, such as *forward, up, down, zigzag, back, forth, round and round*, and so on. Write the words on index cards. Have students each choose a card in turn. Have students show understanding of the word by modeling the action with either their body or an object. After students demonstrate proficiency, add words associated with speed. Have students then model moving objects in a given direction at a given speed.

Beginning Model actions and spoken words, using direction words. For example, *I walk forward.* Invite students to repeat and act out the short sentences.

Intermediate Write simple declarative sentences using direction words from the lesson. Invite partners to choose a sentence to act out for the group. The group then tries to guess the sentence being acted out.

Advanced Have students use direction words to write a simple set of instructions telling how to move from one location in the classroom to another. Have a partner follow the direction statements to check for accuracy.

For All Students Continue the lesson by reminding students to think about the different ways that an object can move.

Extend

Have students complete the **Show What You Know** activity on page 211 to demonstrate their understanding of words that describe direction.

③ Apply and Assess

Play a Direction Word Game

When to Use	Proficiency Levels
With Reading Review p. 503	✔ Beginning
⏱ 20 minutes	✔ Intermediate
	Advanced

- Have students stand in a line.
- Give simple commands using direction words, such as *Walk forward 2 steps.*
- As students follow the directions, redirect and assist as needed.
- Invite students to take turns giving new commands.

Informal Assessment

Beginning	Intermediate	Advanced
Ask students to state one direction word and pantomime the motion, or trace it with their finger. *(Answers will vary, but students should correctly identify a direction word and be able to demonstrate it.)*	Have students choose one direction word and use it to describe a path they could walk in the classroom. Invite them to use the following sentence frame: *I can walk _____.* Have students demonstrate the action in their sentence. *(Answers will vary. Possible answer: I can walk forward.)*	Ask students to write three sentences giving directions from one location in the classroom to another. Tell students to include at least three direction words in their instructions. *(Answers will vary. Possible answer: Walk forward 5 steps. Take 10 steps in a zigzag. Walk backward 4 steps.)*

Direction Words

Draw an arrow in each box to show each direction word.

up	down

round and round	zigzag

 School-Home Connection: Have students take this page home to share with
family members. They can use their pictures to tell about direction words.

© Harcourt

Lesson 2 — What Are Forces?

① Build Background

Access Prior Knowledge

When to Use	Proficiency Levels
Before introducing the lesson 20 minutes	✔ Beginning ✔ Intermediate ✔ Advanced

Materials: toy cars, blocks, small balls, erasers, cans, several books

- Invite students to move the various items on the table.
- Stack the books to create a ramp. Roll items up and down the ramp. Encourage students to do the same, discussing what happens as they move the objects.

Preteach Lesson Vocabulary

> **force, gravity, weight**

List the vocabulary words on the board.

- Bring a chair to the front of the classroom. Invite a volunteer to push the chair as you pantomime. Say *push* aloud. Do the same for pulling the chair, saying *pull*.
- Have students find the word *force* in the lesson. Explain that any kind of push or pull is a *force*. Tell students that a *force* makes things move.
- Point to the word *gravity* on page 510. Tell students that gravity is a force that pulls two objects toward each other. Use your hands to demonstrate two things moving toward each other. Point out that you cannot feel gravity, but if there were no gravity between you and Earth, you would float off into space.
- Ask students if they know how much they weigh. Tell them that *weight* is the way we measure the pull of gravity here on Earth. Objects with more mass weigh more than those with less mass.

Build Fluency

Have students work with a partner by comparing the weight of different objects in the classroom. Invite students to use the following sentence frames to express the results of their comparisons:

The _____ weighs more than the _____.

The _____ weighs less than the _____.

© Harcourt

② Scaffold the Content

Preview the Lesson

When to Use	Proficiency Levels
With pp. 504–510	✔ Beginning
🕐 30 minutes	✔ Intermediate
	✔ Advanced

- Read the lesson title and the Fast Fact aloud.
- Preview the pictures in the lesson, asking students to identify whether each image shows a pushing force or a pulling force.
- Direct students to the lizard on page 507. Point out the words *surface tension* in the caption. Explain that surface tension is a pulling force that creates a kind of skin, or thin layer on the water that the lizard can run on because the lizard does not weigh very much. Ask students to predict if an elephant could run across the water's surface. (No, an elephant is far too heavy to use the surface tension to walk on water.)

Investigate, p. 505

Before students begin the Investigate:

- Write the words *fast*, *faster*, and *fastest* on the board. Gently roll a ball on the floor. Say: "I rolled the ball fast." Roll it again, but slightly faster. Say: "I rolled the ball faster." Finally, roll the ball even faster. Say: "That was the fastest I have rolled the ball."
- Model walking across the room at a slow pace. Say: "I am slow." Invite a volunteer to move across the room more slowly. Say: "_____ is slower." Finally, have a third volunteer walk even more slowly and say: "_____ is the slowest."
- Explain that the words in step 5 compare the speed at which something moves.

Modify Instruction—Multilevel Strategies

Comprehensible Input

- Give partners a ball in a large, open area. Have them use different kinds of force to move the ball. As they move the ball, identify the force they use by saying things like: "That kick was a push. That catch was a pull. That throw was a push."
- Have one student in each pair perform an action with a specific kind of force. For example, say: "Throw the ball softly. Roll the ball fast. Kick the ball hard." Explain that the more force that is used, the faster and farther the object travels.
- Have one student kick the ball as others watch. Explain that the ball begins to slow down because as it rubs against the ground, the force of *friction* slows it down.

Beginning Model examples of pushes and pulls as you verbalize the action. Use *I*, *you*, and *we* in the sentences. Invite students to act out and repeat with you the short sentences.

Intermediate Have students write simple declarative sentences to describe the actions that they performed with the ball. Read aloud the sentences as you underline the action words. Invite students to repeat the sentences and pantomime the actions.

Advanced Have students write one sentence describing an applied force and a second sentence telling how the applied force stopped or changed the direction of the motion. For example: *I kicked the ball. Mary caught the ball.*

For All Students Continue the lesson by reminding students to think about the ways that force can change motion.

Extend

Have students complete the **Show What You Know** activity on page 215 to demonstrate their understanding of how the starting height affects the speed of moving objects.

③ Apply and Assess

Make a Class Mural

When to Use With Reading Review p. 511	Proficiency Levels
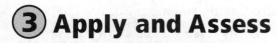 30 minutes	✔ Beginning ✔ Intermediate ✔ Advanced

Materials: butcher paper, crayons

- Review the terms *push* and *pull*. Tell students to think of different ways they can show each type of force. Label *Pushes* on the left side of the paper and *Pulls* on the right side.

- Have each student draw one example of each kind of force and write or dictate simple captions for their drawings.

Informal Assessment

Beginning	Intermediate	Advanced
Give students a ball. Ask them to perform a specific movement with the ball, and to tell how they are moving it. *(Responses will vary but actions and words should agree.)*	Have students copy and complete these sentence frames. Two forces that can make an object move are _____ and _____. _____ is one force that stops things or slows them down. *(Answer: push, pull; friction)*	Ask students to write three sentences, each telling a different type of force and an action that they can take to change or stop the way an object moves. *(Answers will vary but may include sentences with the words* push *and* pull *and* force.*)

© Harcourt

Name _____

Date _____

How Does It Move?

In Box 1, draw a picture of the ramp where your objects moved the fastest.

In Box 2, draw a picture of the ramp where your objects moved the slowest.

On the back, write a sentence telling about the difference between the two ramps.

1

2

School-Home Connection: Have students take this page home to share with family members. They can use their pictures to tell about starting height and speed.

© Harcourt

Lesson 3 How Do Waves Move?

① Build Background

Access Prior Knowledge

When to Use	Proficiency Levels
Before introducing the lesson	✔ Beginning
🕐 20 minutes	✔ Intermediate
	✔ Advanced

Materials: shallow pan of water, pebbles

- Invite students, one at a time, to observe what happens to the water in the pan when a small pebble is dropped into it. Ask them to describe the movement of the water.

- Ask students if they have ever been near a larger body of water like a lake or ocean. Have them describe what the water looked like, sounded like, and how it moved.

Preteach Lesson Vocabulary

> **wave, crest, trough, wavelength**

List the vocabulary words on the board.

- Have students find the word *wave* in the lesson. Ask students to use their arm to pantomime the movement of a wave. Model moving your hand and arm in a wave motion.

- Ask a volunteer to try to draw this motion on the board. Assist the volunteer in creating a wave pattern with multiple crests and troughs.

- Have students find the remaining vocabulary words in the lesson. Read each word and have students echo them.

- Write the words in the appropriate locations to label the wave pattern drawn on the board. Point to the part of the wave and read the label, then have students repeat. When labeling the wavelength, draw a line under the pattern either from crest to crest or from trough to trough. Explain that this distance is the measure of a wavelength.

Build Fluency

Write the following types of waves on the board: *light waves, ocean waves, microwaves, x-rays, sound waves.* Read each type of wave and have students repeat. Then remind students that all waves carry energy. Have students work with a partner to repeat this sentence frame for each type of wave on the board:

_____ carry energy.

© Harcourt

② Scaffold the Content

Preview the Lesson

- After the Fast Fact is read, invite those who have been to an ocean beach to tell how the waves felt and sounded.
- Point to the diagram of the wave on page 514. Explain that a vibration causes movement. Explain that the water in the second picture moves as the wave disturbs it.
- On page 515, point out that sound waves move back and forth, much like the spring toy in the picture.
- The picture on page 516 shows how scientists measure waves. Have students trace their fingers over the crests and troughs as you identify them.

Investigate, p. 513

Before students begin the Investigate:

- Review with students the direction words *up* and *down*. Pantomime how students will move their arms in order to achieve an up and down movement with the rope. Explain that students will start by only moving a little to achieve a *gentle* motion. Then students will move the rope a bit faster.
- Before students complete step 3, review the movements of *push* and *pull*. Demonstrate the distance that students should push the toy toward their partner.

Modify Instruction—Multilevel Strategies

Comprehensible Input

Materials: tuning fork, pan of water

- Help students to better understand the concept of waves through the following simple demonstrations. Have students place their fingers on their throats. Then invite them to hum a low note and describe what they feel. Explain that they are feeling the vibration of their vocal cords that makes sound.
- Strike a tuning fork and have students observe both vibrations and resulting sound. Strike the fork again, and place the tip of the fork in a pan of water. Explain that the energy of sound causes the water to move.

Beginning Have students draw a simple wave pattern. Name and point to the *crest*, *trough*, and *wavelength* as students follow along. Then help students to trace with their finger the path that energy travels along a wavelength.

© Harcourt

Intermediate Have students describe one way they can show wave formation. Then have them demonstrate it.

Advanced Have students choose one demonstration that showed the formation of waves. Ask them to draw a picture of how the wave moved and write a short description of what happened to form the wave.

For All Students Continue to help students identify the different types of waves and then guide them to see how waves are measured.

Extend

Have students complete the **Show What You Know** activity on page 219 to demonstrate their understanding of the parts of a wave and how a wave is measured.

③ Apply and Assess

Make a Word Web

When to Use With Reading Review p. 517 🕐 20 minutes	Proficiency Levels ✔ Beginning ✔ Intermediate ✔ Advanced

- Write the word *wave* in the center of a word web.

- Have students recall words they learned in the lesson that are related to waves.

- Classify student responses into categories, such things as *kinds of waves*, *parts of a wave*, *ways to create waves*, *measuring waves*, or other appropriate categories.

- Invite students to work with a partner to explain each word on the web and tell how it relates to waves.

Informal Assessment

Beginning	Intermediate	Advanced
Show students a diagram of a wave pattern. Say: "Find the crest." Have students point to the correct part and name it. Repeat for *trough* and *wavelength*. (*Students should point to and name the correct parts of the wave.*)	Give students a tuning fork and ask them to show a wave vibration. Then have them tell why the wave happened. (*Student should strike the tuning fork to show a wave vibration. Then the student should explain that the wave occurred because the tuning fork was struck, causing it to move or vibrate.*)	Have students complete the following sentence frames. *Waves disturb matter by causing it to _____. Waves carry _____.* (*Answers: move; energy*)

© Harcourt

Name _____

Date _____

Parts of a Wave

Label the **crest**, **trough**, and **wavelength** on this wave pattern. On the back, write at least three different kinds of waves.

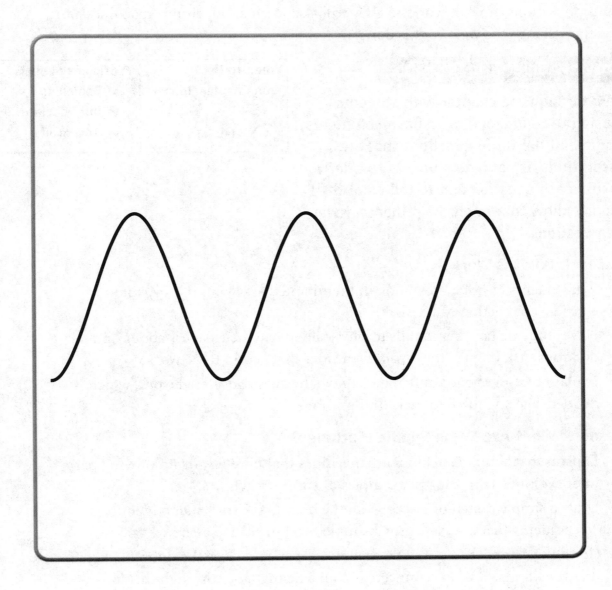

School-Home Connection: Have students take this page home to share with family members. They can use their pictures to tell about waves.

© Harcourt

16 Work and Machines

Develop Scientific Concepts and Vocabulary

In this chapter, students will learn how the scientific concept of work differs from common notions of what work is. They will also learn about simple machines and how they change the way work is done.

Preview Scientific Principles

Walk through the chapter with students, pausing to read aloud or to have volunteers read aloud the three questions that are lesson titles. Encourage students to briefly discuss each question and to tell what they already know that might help them answer the questions.

When to Use With Chapter Opener	Proficiency Levels
20 minutes	✔ Beginning ✔ Intermediate ✔ Advanced

Lesson 1: What Is Work?

- Ask students to hold a textbook in their hands. Ask them if they would consider that action to be work.

- Have students use their hands to physically move their papers about on their desktops. Ask them if they would consider that action to be work.

- Explain that in science only the second activity is considered work, which is defined as using force to make things move.

Lesson 2: What Are Some Simple Machines?

- Explain that simple machines are machines that have few or no moving parts. Invite volunteers to suggest examples of simple machines.

- Draw a simple sketch of a seesaw on the board. Ask students to identify it. Tell students that a seesaw uses a simple machine called a *lever*.

- Go to the classroom door, turn the knob, open and close the door. Explain that the knob is a wheel connected to an axle that goes through the door. This is another simple machine.

- Draw a simple sketch of an old-fashioned well with bucket, rope, and pulley. Explain how the bucket is lowered into the well to retrieve water. Point out the pulley, another simple machine.

Lesson 3: What Are Some Other Simple Machines?

- Ask students whether it is easier to climb a cliff or walk up a hill. Explain that it is easier to walk up a hill because a hill is an inclined plane, a type of simple machine.

- Have students place one hand on the desktop with fingers held tightly together. Then have them force one finger of the other hand between two fingers of the first hand, forcing them apart. Explain that they have just used that one finger as a wedge, another type of simple machine.

- Find a screw that is used somewhere in the classroom. Have students examine it. Explain that it is another form of simple machine that is used to do work.

Practice

To help students use vocabulary from the chapter's topic, involve them in contributing to a giant word web around the central word *work* on the board. Encourage students to dictate or write related words around the focus word. Words might be *hard*, *difficult*, *movement*, *action*, etc.

Then have students choose words from the web to use in sentences about work. Encourage them to read their sentences aloud.

Apply

Write a list of the six simple machines on the board and have students take turns echoing or reading them and summarizing what they do. Then ask them to search old magazines for pictures of things that use simple machines. Have them cut and paste the pictures on a sheet of paper to create a collage poster.

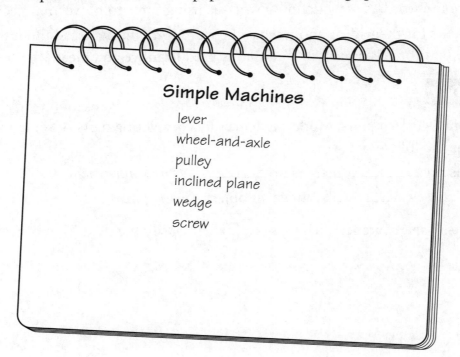

Simple Machines

lever
wheel-and-axle
pulley
inclined plane
wedge
screw

Lesson 1 What Is Work?

① Build Background

Access Prior Knowledge

When to Use	Proficiency Levels
Before introducing the lesson	✔ Beginning
⏱ 15 minutes	✔ Intermediate
	Advanced

- Give students an opportunity to use sentences as they talk about their ideas about work.
- Ask them to give examples of work they have done or work they have seen others do.
- Ask them what work does.

Preteach Lesson Vocabulary

> work

Materials: book

Write the vocabulary word on the board.

Have students look at page 530 and look for the word on the board. Then:

- Ask for a volunteer to stand with you in front of the group.
- Place a book on a desk and ask the volunteer to pick up the book and move it from one end of the desk to the other.
- Tell the group that what they have just seen is an example of what scientists call work.
- Introduce the word *force* by defining work as using force to move an object.
- Ask students for their ideas about what the word *force* means. Lead them to conclude that force is a push or pull that is used to move an object.

Build Fluency

Have students work in pairs. Model sentences by completing pairs of sentence frames such as the following:

1. If there is no _____, there is no _____. *(force, movement)*
2. _____ uses _____ to move an object. *(work, force)*

Ask students to use sentences like these to further clarify the definition of work.

② Scaffold the Content

Preview the Lesson

Ask students to point to the title on page 526 as you read it aloud. Explain to them that they will find the answer to this question in the lesson. Ask students to tell about work they have done that has also been fun.

Next, ask students to look at the pictures on pages 527 through 532, and to tell about any similarities or differences they see among the pictures.

- Explain that some of the pictures show work being done, while others do not.
- Point out that the words *force* and *move* are details that tell more about work.
- Write *measure* on the board. Have students find it on page 527. Discuss the word.
- Ask students why measuring is important in determining whether work has been done.

Investigate, p. 527

Before the students begin the Investigate, help students understand *checker* and *checkerboard* by teaching them how to play checkers. Then have students work with partners to complete the Investigate.

Ask students to tell what they did to complete the activity. Help them draw conclusions by asking volunteers to answer aloud the activity questions.

You might want to build comprehension and provide meaning for other important technical words, such as *measure* and *solve*. Read aloud each word you choose, use it in a context sentence, and provide its meaning. Then, have students find it in their texts.

Modify Instruction—Multilevel Strategies

Background/Experience The concept of work involves understanding that work uses force to move things. The following activities provide opportunities for students to recognize examples of work in their own daily lives.

Beginning Have the students draw pictures of themselves performing some daily chore or activity. Ask them to show their pictures and describe how work is being performed in the picture. Remind them to remember the concepts of force and movement.

Intermediate Have students copy from the board simple sentences about work, force, and movement. Read each sentence aloud, having students read along or echo the sentences. Then, have students act out their sentences for the group to guess.

© Harcourt

Advanced Ask students to turn to page 531. Call on volunteers to read the captions. Then call on volunteers to answer the questions. Encourage discussion of the answers.

For All Students Direct students to the pictures on page 532. Remind students to think about work, force, and movement. Ask volunteers to identify the picture showing work.

Extend

Have the students complete the **Show What You Know** activity on page 225 to demonstrate their understanding of the scientific definition of work.

③ Apply and Assess

Make a Picture Display

When to Use	Proficiency Levels
With Reading Review p. 533 ⏱ 20 minutes	✔ Beginning ✔ Intermediate ✔ Advanced

Materials: magazines, scissors, paper, paste

- Have students work together in groups of three to five to find and cut out magazine pictures that show work.
- Have them organize the pictures by the type of work being performed.
- Ask the groups to paste the pictures that display similar types of work on a sheet of paper and to label the page with words that describe the work.

Informal Assessment

Beginning	Intermediate	Advanced
Have each student give an example of a type of work. *(Answers will vary.)*	Have each student give an example of a way force can produce movement. *(Answers will vary.)*	Have each student write two sentences. Each sentence should describe how force produces movement in a type of work. *(Answers will vary.)*

© Harcourt

Name _____

Date _____

Describing Work

Use words from the list to fill in the blanks.

work	force	motion	measure

1. _____ is what happens when _____

   causes _____.

2. There are ways to _____ how much

   _____ has been done.

School-Home Connection: Have students take this page home to share with family members. They can use their sentences to tell about work.

Lesson 2 — What Are Some Simple Machines?

① Build Background

Access Prior Knowledge

When to Use	Proficiency Levels
Before introducing the lesson 🕐 15 minutes	✔ Beginning ✔ Intermediate Advanced

- Give students an opportunity to use sentences as they talk about simple machines.
- Ask them to give examples of simple machines they have used or simple machines they have seen others use.
- Ask them what simple machines are for.

Preteach Lesson Vocabulary

> simple machine, lever, fulcrum, wheel-and-axle, pulley

Materials: book, ruler

List the vocabulary words on the board.

Have students look at page 538 and look for any words on the board. Then:

- Ask for a volunteer. Place a book on top of a ruler on a desk with half the ruler sticking out, and ask the volunteer to pick up the protruding end of the ruler. Tell the group to observe what happens to the book.
- Tell the group that what they have just seen is an example of a simple machine, in this case a lever, in action.
- Introduce the word *fulcrum* by defining a fulcrum as the fixed point on a lever.
- Ask students for their ideas about what served as the fulcrum in the demonstration (the desk top). Lead them to conclude that levers and fulcrums work together to do work.

Build Fluency

Have students work in pairs. Model sentences by completing pairs of sentence frames such as the following:

1. A _____ is a bar that pivots. *(lever)*
2. A _____ is the fixed point on a lever. *(fulcrum)*

Ask students to use sentences like these to further clarify the definition of *lever*.

© Harcourt

② Scaffold the Content

Preview the Lesson

When to Use With pp. 534–542	Proficiency Levels
15 minutes	✔ Beginning ✔ Intermediate ✔ Advanced

Ask students to point to the title on page 534 as you read it aloud. Explain to them that they will find the answer to this question in the lesson. Have students discuss the picture. Ask students to give their ideas about what simple machines are. Encourage them to give examples of simple machines they think they may have used.

Next ask students to look at the pictures on pages 536 through 542, and to tell about any similarities or differences they see among the pictures.

- Explain that the pictures show different kinds of simple machines.
- Point out that a machine is anything that changes the way work is done.
- Write *simple machine* on the board. Have students find it on page 537. Discuss it.
- Ask students how a simple machine like a rake differs from a machine like a leafblower.

Investigate, p. 535

Before the students begin the Investigate, allow them to examine and use a tablespoon and a forceps to pick up wild and white rice. Then have students complete the Investigate.

Ask students to tell what they did to complete the activity. Help them draw conclusions by asking volunteers to answer aloud the activity questions.

You might want to build comprehension and provide meaning for other important technical words, such as *engine*, *pivot*, and *shank*. Read aloud each word you choose, use it in a context sentence, and provide its meaning. Then have students find it in their texts.

Modify Instruction—Multilevel Strategies

Comprehensible Input The concept of simple machines involves understanding that a simple machine has few or no moving parts. The following activities provide opportunities for students to recognize examples of simple machines in their own daily lives.

Beginning Have the students draw pictures of themselves or family members performing some daily chore or activity. Have them show their pictures and tell whether or not they are using a simple machine in the picture.

Intermediate Have students copy simple sentences from the board about simple machines. Read each sentence aloud, having students read along or echo the sentences.

Advanced Draw a circle and write in it "Simple Machines." Draw three circles outside of this circle. Have students copy this graphic organizer and write the name of a simple machine in each outer circle, along with several tools that use the simple machine.

For All Students Direct the students to the picture on page 541. Remind students to think of simple machines as having few or no moving parts. Then, call on volunteers to identify the wheel (handle) and axle (shank) of the screwdriver.

Extend

Have the students complete the **Show What You Know** activity on page 229 to demonstrate their ability to visually recognize various simple machines.

③ Apply and Assess

Make a Mural

When to Use With Reading Review p. 543 🕐 30 minutes	Proficiency Levels ✔ Beginning ✔ Intermediate ✔ Advanced

Materials: paper for drawing murals, colored pencils or crayons

- Have students work in groups of three to five to create a mural of simple machines.
- Have them draw pictures of the simple machines, label them by name and explain, in caption form, the function and uses of each simple machine.
- Display the finished murals on the walls of the classroom and have student groups present their murals to the rest of the class. Discuss how the murals are similar or different.

Informal Assessment

Beginning	Intermediate	Advanced
Have each student give an example of a type of simple machine. *(Answers will vary.)*	Have each student give an example of the work a certain type of simple machine can do. *(Answers will vary.)*	Have each student write two sentences. Each sentence should describe how a certain type of simple machine changes the way work is done. *(Answers will vary.)*

© Harcourt

Name _____

Date _____

Matching Tools with Simple Machines

Draw lines to match the tools on the left with the simple machines on the right.

arm of nutcracker   lever and fulcrum

doorknob   wheel-and-axle

well with bucket   pulley

screwdriver

shovel

flagpole with flag

School-Home Connection: Have students take this page home to share with family members. They can find examples of simple machines around the home to compare with the ones on the page.

Lesson 3

What Are Some Other Simple Machines?

1 Build Background

Access Prior Knowledge

When to Use	Proficiency Levels
Before introducing the lesson	✔ Beginning
🕐 15 minutes	✔ Intermediate
	Advanced

- Give students an opportunity to use sentences as they talk about simple machines.
- Ask them to give examples of simple machines they have used or simple machines they have seen others use.
- Ask them if they can name some of these simple machines.

Preteach Lesson Vocabulary

> **inclined plane, wedge, screw**

List the vocabulary words on the board.

Have students look at page 546 and look for any words on the board. Then:

- Have a volunteer read the words on the board out loud.
- Invite students to offer definitions of the words on the board.
- Call on other volunteers to come to the board and draw simple sketches.

Build Fluency

Have students work in pairs. Model sentences by completing pairs of sentence frames such as the following:

1. An _____ is like a slope. *(inclined plane)*
2. An _____ makes moving and lifting things easier. *(inclined plane)*

Ask students to use sentences like these to further clarify the definition of an inclined plane.

© Harcourt

② Scaffold the Content

When to Use	Proficiency Levels
With pp. 544–550 15 minutes	✔ Beginning ✔ Intermediate ✔ Advanced

Preview the Lesson

Ask students to point to the title on page 544 as you read it aloud. Explain to them that they will find the answer to this question in the lesson. Have students discuss the picture. Ask students to give their ideas about what some other simple machines might be.

Next, ask students to look at the pictures on pages 546 through 550, and to tell about any similarities or differences they see among the pictures.

- Explain that the pictures show different kinds of simple machines.
- Point out that these simple machines are similar to those in Lesson 2 in that they have few or no moving parts.
- Write *ramp* on the board. Have students find it on page 547. Discuss the word.
- Ask students how a ramp makes it easier to raise heavy objects.

Investigate, p. 545

Before the students begin the Investigate, pass a spring scale around to students to examine at close hand. Explain the use and function of the spring scale. Show the difference between vertical distance and distance up a ramp. Then have students complete the Investigate.

Ask students to tell what they did to complete the activity. Help them draw conclusions by asking volunteers to answer aloud the activity questions.

You might want to build comprehension for other important technical words, such as *axe*, *chisel*, and *nail*. Read aloud each word you choose, use it in a context sentence, and provide its meaning. Then have students find it in their texts.

Modify Instruction—Multilevel Strategies

Language/Vocabulary Introduce the concept of words with multiple meanings using the word *plane* as an example. Explain that as it is used in the phrase *inclined plane*, it means a surface. It also is short for airplane, and it also is a type of tool used for shaving wood.

Beginning Have students draw pictures of inclined planes and airplanes. Ask them if there are any similarities between the two. Point out that although the two objects are represented by the same word, the objects are not related in any way.

© Harcourt

Intermediate Write several multiple meaning words on the board. Read the words aloud and give their meanings as students repeat after you. Then have students select and define words in their own terms.

Advanced Ask students to find other multiple meaning words in the lesson (*direct, hard, gentle, thread*). Have students pick words and give the meanings of the words, first as they are used in the lesson, then as they are used in another way.

For All Students Ask students to turn to page 546. Call on volunteers to read the illustration captions. Then call on volunteers to tell what is being moved in the example of the slope up the mountain. Encourage discussion of the answers to the questions.

Extend

Have the students complete the **Show What You Know** activity on page 233 to demonstrate their understanding of inclined planes, wedges, and screws.

③ Apply and Assess

When to Use	Proficiency Levels
With Reading Review p. 551	✔ Beginning
	✔ Intermediate
20 minutes	✔ Advanced

Put On a Skit

- Have students work in groups of three to five to create brief skits in which they pantomime using inclined planes, wedges, and screws.
- Have other students guess what each skit was intended to represent.

Informal Assessment

Beginning	Intermediate	Advanced
Have each student give an example of an inclined plane, a wedge, or a screw. *(Answers will vary.)*	Have each student give an example of the work done by one of these three simple machines. *(Answers will vary.)*	Have each student write two sentences. Each sentence should describe how one of these three types of simple machines changes the way work is done. *(Answers will vary.)*

Defining More Simple Machines

Write the definition of each simple machine. Then draw a picture of it in the box.

1. inclined slope

_____

_____

_____

2. wedge

_____

_____

_____

3. screw

_____

_____

_____

School-Home Connection: Have students take this page home to share with
family members. They can use it to show family members what they have learned
about these three simple machines.

© Harcourt